Glen Turlock

This regis
access t

MW01098842

Please complete a

detach and mail
as soon as you wish to visit us "on-line."

Upon reception of your registration card, we will
send you an E-mail with:

a special Site Address

a Username

and a Password

which will give you full access to
our site and its related services.

We will not accept photocopies of this document.

PLEASE DETACH HERE

PLEASE DETACH ON THIS LINE

Registration Authorization #: L@L - 732 - 475987635

Please complete the following information.

Name: _____

E-mail: _____ @_____

Postal code/Zip: _____

**Unfortunately, incomplete information will not
allow us to validate your access to our site.**

In order to activate
the web site you must mail the
registration card below.

PLEASE
AFFIX
POSTAGE
HERE

Learning@living

PO Box 413
1027 Davie Street
Vancouver, BC V6E4L2
Canada

Learning@living

A LIVING book . . .
www.living-icic.com

Mike Bourcier
& Michèle Lévesque

Seattle, Washington
Portland, Oregon
Denver, Colorado
Vancouver, B.C.

ISBN: 0-89716-673-6

LCC: 96-071307

01.0126

Cover Design: David Marty

Editing & Production: Christi Scattarella

First printing January 1997

10 9 8 7 6 5 4 3 2 1

Peanut Butter Publishing
226 2nd Avenue West • Seattle, WA 98119 • 206-281-5965
Old Post Office Bldg. • 510 S.W. 3rd • Portland, OR 97201
Cherry Creek • 50 S. Steele • Suite 850 • Denver, CO 80209
Su. 230 1333 Johnston St. Pier 32 Granville Isl., Vancouver, B.C. V6H 3R9
e mail: P NUT PUB@aol.com
http://www.pbpublishing.com

Printed in Canada

CONTENTS

A living book ...

about **NOT** "living" to work
about "working" to live
about "earning" just reward
about "learning" to live
about "learning" to learn
about "making" a living
about "life" itself

INTRODUCTION

When we set out to write this book, Michèle and I realized that as we approached fifty, our lives were not getting any easier. It felt as if we had worked ourselves into a corner with tremendous obligations and commitments. In fact, we were at a point where we spent most of our time managing our lives instead of enjoying them, just at a time when things should have gotten easier.

We had met in 1989, both coming out of marriages that were not meeting our expectations after several years. I had two grown children; Michèle had none. We were both professionals looking for a new orientation. Our different skills were complementary, so was our outlook on the future. The divorces had wiped us out financially, and we accepted this as a necessary evil. We had started to rebuild our lives separately at first and together as we married in 1991.

We started our journey to re-learn to earn a living about eighteen months prior to the publication of this book. And what an interesting time we had. The first shock was that the most difficult part of our journey was not the beginning. What surprised us most was the realization that in order to learn a living, we had to "unlearn" what we knew and took for granted. The unlearning process made us examine our Values and Beliefs about virtually everything, from our definition of success to our appreciation of failure, from our distorted dependence on money to the true meaning of happiness.

2

"People waste
more time waiting
for someone to
take charge of their
lives than they do
in any other pursuit"
   - Gloria Steinem

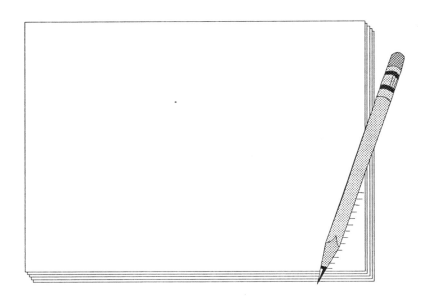

During this expedition, we got lost; we became distracted. Then we found our way back to the right road, discovering ourselves individually and as a couple. Being impatient, we wanted to see results at each step along the way. We developed our own tools to evaluate the process and made decisions as we progressed toward our goals. This constant reinforcement provided us with the validation we needed to persist.

As our Learning@living adventure got underway, we began to rethink many of the material trappings that we once deemed necessities. We ultimately found the house of our dreams, a log cabin in the Canadian Rockies. The house belongs more to us than it does the bank, a nice change. We altered our business set-up dramatically. We moved an international operation from traditional offices into a home office. Our company, The International Consortium of Independent Consultants (ICIC) Inc., regroups more than 30 consultants from 20 countries. Michele and I offer seminars on advanced communication skills in Canada, the U.S. and Europe. We are on retainer with large organizations and Governments to develop senior management teams and help people facing change and downsizing in setting-up a new course in earning a living. By simplifying, we now live quite comfortably on twenty percent of our former income and we have more quality time for each other as a couple.

It didn't take too long before our friends and acquaintances started asking questions about the significant changes in our lives. We ended-up sharing our experience with others regularly. Then, of course, came the idea of a book.

"Everything
    has been figured
        out except
        how to live."

- Jean-Paul Sarte

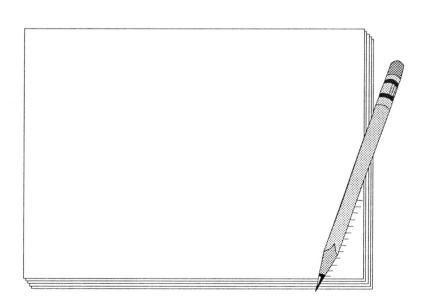

But a book is a book, and there are so many on shelves gathering dust. The question was: "How can we make a difference in the lives of people and provide them with information and support that is always up-to-date in a world that is changing every six months?" The answer: "A living book!"

With today's technology, we were able to conceive a book that dispenses information in a dynamic way using the Internet as a means to keep it alive. In addition, a living book allows the reader to share his/her experience with other readers and offers "on-line" advice, assessment tools and instruments that are kept current. The next section: "How to use this book" is self-explanatory and will be clear even to the technophobe. If you are not yet "on the Net" you can still greatly benefit from the contents of this book. We hope that we will be contributing to your desire to join the Cyber-community.

"Learning@living" is about learning to earn a living. It is also about learning to learn and learning to live. Our old beliefs about family, money and work are not taking us very far in our quest to create the life that we want. In "The Last Book you'll ever read," Frank Ogden says: "As this bulldozer of change rolls over our planet we have a choice: to become part of the bulldozer or part of the road." The skills we will need to ride this bulldozer continue to evolve. We need to embrace a new approach toward learning if we want to "stay on top." Learning is not an alternative, it is a must.

"The man who doesn't read good books has no advantage over the man who can't read."

- Mark Twain

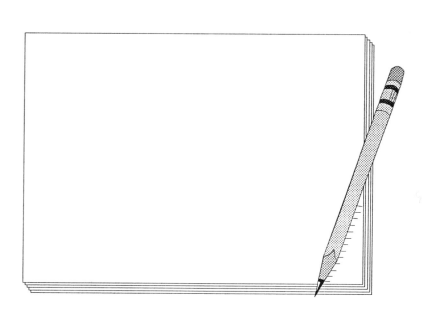

Along the same line of thought, earning a living does not necessarily mean accruing money to afford a lifestyle. In many cases, as you will see in this book, people have chosen lifestyles and found resources other than money that made their dream come true.

Earning a living is about "having earned" your lifestyle. Some people will "earn" a good retirement because of wise investments that guarantee them a sufficient level of income that, in turn, assures them the lifestyle they desire. Others who relied on pension plans that now barely put food on the table are forced to rethink their needs. They must continue to "earn" their living way past their anticipated date of retirement. Even that word "retirement" does not carry the connotation it once did. People who retire at fifty-five are now looking at another ten to fifteen years of a second or third career.

As we approach the next millennium, learning has begun to take on a new meaning. Vertical career paths are rapidly disappearing. As of this day, the failing education system has yet to address the new dimension of work. We were molded to believe that choosing a career at an early age and sticking to it through years of schooling would provide us with gainful employment at the end of our ordeal. We thought there was only one right answer, the one provided by our educators. What we find now is that there is no single correct answer. Consequently, many of us had to get used to "gray" instead of black and white. Everything is a shade of gray and there are an infinite array of hues.

"Good judgment
comes from
experience
which comes from
bad judgment."

- Unknown

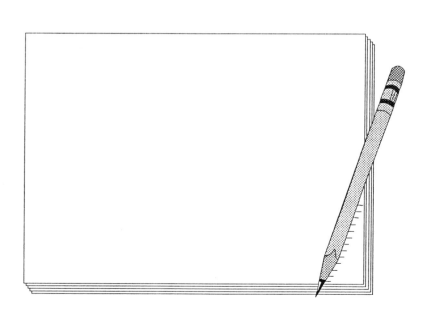

Learning@living is more than a book. It is a resource center with live examples, simple processes, working documents and instruments that will provide you with the support you need to realize your goals. It will remain up-to-date and continue to offer leading edge advice for years. It can guide you in a very personal way or afford you the opportunity to share your experiences anonymously or not with others.

As a resource center, Learning@living had to provide the best available advice in all areas. For this reason, we have sought the opinions of experts in many fields. We would like to mention a special effort from our friends and business acquaintances, David Melles and Cory Wade, whose expertise in personal financial planning has been invaluable. David and Cory have designed and developed the section on finances presented in this book.

We hope you enjoy the journey as much as we have.

Mike Bourcier and Michèle Lévesque

"The way a book is read-
which is to say the qualities a
reader brings to a book-
can have as much to do
with its worth
as anything
the author puts into it."
-Norman Cousins

HOW TO USE THIS BOOK

By itself, this book will serve as a companion for your journey. We are providing you with simple and effective tools and worksheets that will guide your journey towards Learning@living. In addition, you will quickly realize that once you access its "home page" on the Internet, its power to serve you is awesome.

Before we proceed further, we would like to tell you that we made a few assumptions about the technology.

We assumed that the reader of this book who wants to access its full power on the Internet has the following:

✓ A computer, a mouse and a printer

✓ A telephone, a modem and an Internet Service Provider

✓ An E-mail account

✓ A browser like "Internet Explorer" or "Netscape"

✓ Enough knowledge to type in our WWW address
  and access our page

Like any other book, this one has its own format and protocols:

> The right pages contain all the text in a continuous form.

Worksheets

Instruments

Exercises

Quotations

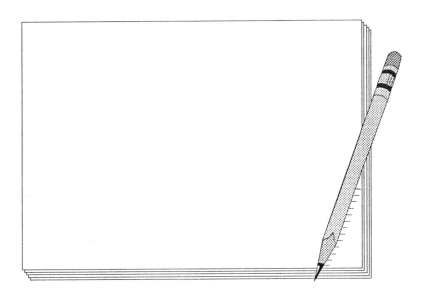

... and lots of space to record your thoughts.

The left pages contain any worksheet or exercise requiring your input along with quotations we offer for your enjoyment and lots of space to record your thoughts.

Learning@living uses the Internet as an additional tool to provide you with up-to-date knowledge, information and connection to others on the same journey. We have adopted the international World Wide Web (WWW) protocol to highlight the linkages between the book and its site.

The entire book is available to read and consult "on-line." It is displayed in the same format, page for page. Retrieving additional tools and instruments is easy as you only have to access the same chapter you're reading and scroll down to the desired page.

Any underlined word, group of words or sentence indicates that by "clicking" on this word while "on-line," you will be taken to another location on our site or somewhere on the WWW to get additional information. In some instances, "clicking" on the word will display additional information.

Once "on-line," follow the instructions you receive. To see the content of the "opposite page" you simply "click" the button that says: "Go to opposite page." Some documents are available to print or save as a file. Other instruments take you through a step-by-step questionnaire to be compiled by the computer. Results from these interactive tests and instruments appear immediately on your screen or will be E-mailed to you within a few minutes.

World Wide Web site:

www.living-icic.com

E-mail:

learning@living-icic.com

Automatic updates
Search engines
Chat Lines
Usergroups

Coaching/support through:
E-mail
Internet Phone
Video Conferencing

In some cases, you will be invited to participate in "Usergroup" discussions, using your E-mail. In other cases, you may choose to join "Live Chat Lines" where you can entertain "keyboard" discussions with others.

For those of you with advanced equipment, you may decide to participate to "Live Voice Conferences" or schedule a video-conference with Michèle and I. We designed the interface with users in mind. It is simple and you will grow with it.

Ongoing additions of material to the book will be posted in a "What's new?" section and/or will be sent to you by E-mail if you elected to receive our updates.

Learning@living will not need a sequel. It will be "alive" and will change as things change around us. You are part of this process. Your input, ideas and comments are invaluable to us and others. Our readers are the life-blood that will keep this book "alive."

Let us begin the journey.

"To be independent
of public opinion is
the first formal
condition of
achieving
anything great."
    - G.W.F. Hegel

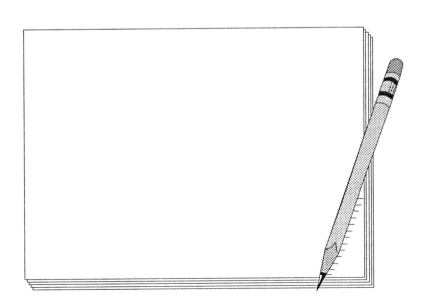

VALUES

What are your three most important values?

If you had to answer this question immediately, without giving it much thought, what would the answer be? Would you have difficulty arriving at an answer instantly? Most of us would need a few minutes to reflect on the critical values that shape our lives.

Do we live our lives based on these most significant values? If someone was to ask the people who know you best what values you live by, would they answer as you have? Is it possible that our behavior contradicts our values?

Where do values come from?

If we look back, can we remember how and when our values became such a vital part of who we are?

The first influence, for most of us, was learning right from wrong from our parents. For many, the church and the school expanded on this most basic value. Yet as we grew, our peers often tested our convictions by challenging us to act contrary to what we believed in. In order to belong, we frequently succumbed to our peers. More influence came from advertising, television shows, politicians, and our submission to authority.

"I will work in my own way according to the light that is in me."

- Lydia Maria Child

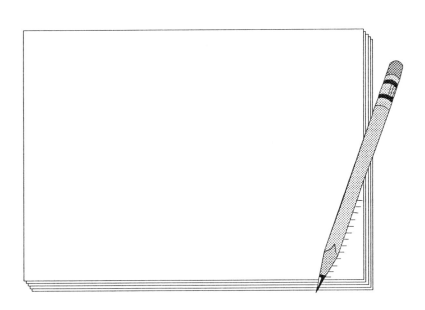

In the midst of this turmoil, some of us made no conclusion whatsoever and just went with the flow, drifting like a ship without a rudder. If we acknowledge being part of this group, we know that our actions and decisions reflect this lack of direction; looking back at our route thus far, we can identify several shifts in direction that ultimately led us nowhere.

We might also notice that these shifts coincided with our association with people who have had a strong positive or negative influence on our lives.

The value clarification exercise that we will do next concerns the present and the future. It might also be useful to glance briefly at the past as we understand how two conflicting values may have contributed to our struggle, to our feeling of being pulled in opposing directions when making some important decision. What's important to remember is that we always have the capacity to change. Reflecting on the past events of our lives is an effective exercise that helps us understand in a tangible way the specific values that have been driving us thus far.

Each choice we make is based on our value system. Whenever we encounter a difficult decision, we must take a step back and verify if our hesitation is based on a value conflict. If it is, understanding that duality is the first step toward reaching an internal resolution.

A friend of ours was extremely unhappy in his job. We had known him for years as a pleasant optimistic person, as long as we steered clear of discussing his employment.

"We can secure other people's approval if we do it right and try hard; but our own is worth a hundred of it."

- Mark Twain

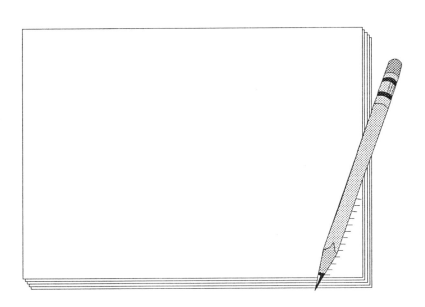

Still, we did not realize how unhappy he was until we stayed at his house for a few days.

The first morning, we had coffee with him before he left for work. It was troubling to hear his despondent tone and realize how bad he felt. You would have guessed that he was on his way to a funeral. The evenings were much better as he attended to his family and hobbies and he never talked about his day at work. After a few days of observing his depressed attitude in the mornings, we decided to help and sat down with he and his wife to discuss the matter.

He was torn inside because, as he put it, he "didn't have the guts" to leave the job he hated, and this was obviously affecting his self-esteem. Together, we explored why and realized that **at this time in his life**, his most important value was his children, more specifically his children's education. One child was entering college, and the two others were not far behind. Making a move that could potentially jeopardize his finances was not an option.

He came to realize that he remained in a position that displeased him not because he was a weakling, but because he valued his family. Once he understood that he had made an honorable choice, the relief he felt was immediately apparent in his facial expression. Of course, the discussion proceeded so that we could help him find ways to benefit more from his work and begin **now** to prepare for a second career that would begin once his children graduated.

It becomes even more complex when we have to make joint decisions with a spouse, for instance.

"I believe that anyone can conquer fear by doing the things he fears to do, provided he keeps doing them until he gets a record of successful experience behind him."

- Eleanore Roosevelt

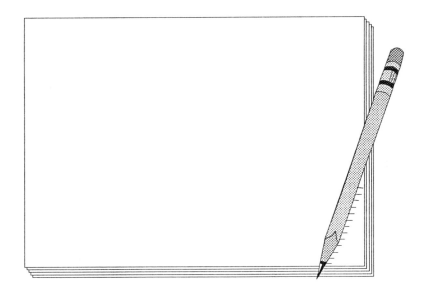

Chances are, that in choosing a life partner, we unconsciously are attracted to people who share or have similar values, but that is not always the case. Understanding and respecting the fact that we will react differently because of our long-standing values is the first step toward reaching agreement and maintaining a harmonious relationship.

If our values are well defined and clear, we will not succumb to pressure, we will not procrastinate for weeks, months and even years, feeling inadequate and incongruent. We will be able to say to ourselves and to others: "I have decided to do... for the following reason...."

Others may not always understand, some will pass judgment on us. It is very difficult to accept the fact that the people we care about have totally different and sometimes even possess value systems diametrically opposed to our own. We attempt to transfer our value system to our children and the intention is good, after all, this is our code of conduct, what we believe is right. Inasmuch as we try to guide them through the confusion of the teenage years into adulthood, ultimately, each person must choose values for him or herself. The following examples will feel familiar to some of you:

✓ Your children decide to travel the world with a backpack, doing odd jobs, for a few years.

*How do you react if your primary value is **security**?*

"No man is a failure who is enjoying life."

- William Feather

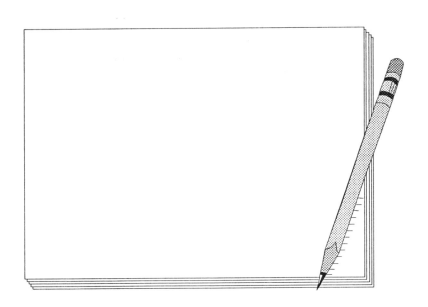

✓ They elect not to have children, they prefer two careers and material abundance.

> *How does this sound to someone who values **family** above all else?*

✓ They leave a secure job to start a risky business.

> *What if **failure** is the ultimate torment for you?*

✓ You are offered a fantastic opportunity that promises excitement and growth but you have to leave a good paying job to grab it... Nonetheless you take it.

> *How do your **conservative** parents react?*

✓ You are extremely unhappy in your failing marriage and you are getting a divorce.

> *How does this sound to your relatives who believe that when you make a **commitment** you stand by it, no matter what!*

If we don't understand, does this mean we have failed as parents? If they don't understand does it mean that they don't care about our feelings? What about our friends, our co-workers? What lies at the root of their bewildering behaviors?

When we devote time and effort to discuss values with people we care about, with business partners, within work teams, it becomes much easier to understand and not judge.

"He who has begun
has half done.

Dare to be wise;
begin!"

- Horace 658 BC

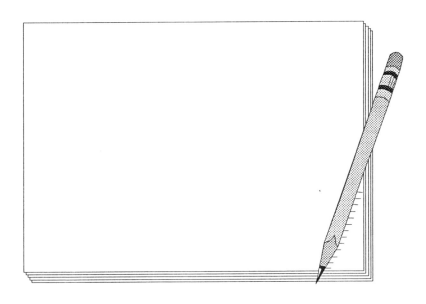

A very important lesson.

As consultants to large organizations, we are often asked to determine which employee is best suited for a certain position. We have learned the hard way, very early on, that without an open discussion about values, we tread on uncertain ground.

In one instance, after interviewing and assessing the background of fifteen managers, we made a recommendation to a Director to promote Jim to a much higher position. In our opinion, he was the best choice. During the interviews, we realized that he was held in high esteem by external clients and co-workers, his work was outstanding, he was at the office at 7:00 every morning. The promotion was offered and he accepted.

A few months later, our client, the director, called us back and informed us that Jim was not working out. Jim seemed very unhappy and his performance was deteriorating.

Puzzled, we asked him out for coffee. He explained that despite his excitement over the new position, his new duties infringed on his family life. The reason he would arrive at 7:00 a.m. for work was that it enabled him to leave the office in time to take his sons to hockey practice at 4:00 in the afternoon. Now he was stuck in meetings late into the day.

Some of us may think: "Come on! Hockey practice, be serious!" Others among us may understand. It is a question of values. **At this moment in his life,** Jim's top value was his family, his desire to be a part of his children's activities.

"To be a nobody,
do nothing!"

- B.C. Forbes

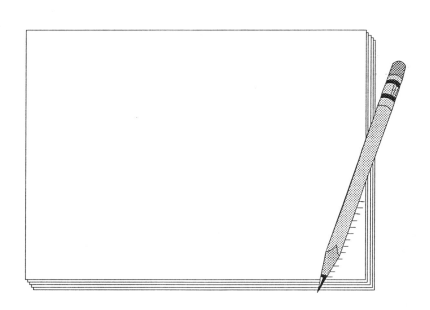

If his job separated him from what he valued most, he would become conflicted, pulled in two different directions. If the tug-of-war between commitment to work and commitment to family went on long enough, he could very likely become sick.

Of course, his career was also an important value, but it was lower in the hierarchy. This is why positioning your values in order of importance is critical.

We sat with the Director and went back to the drawing board, admitting we had made a mistake, sharing with her the very important lesson we had just learned. By the way, Jim kept his new position and arrangements were made to accommodate his needs. Originally, he thought that going to his boss to tell her that hockey practice was important to him was a career limiting move. He was fortunate to deal with a manager who understood and respected the values of others. He had enough "value" in the organization to warrant an exception to the rules.

What is a value?

A value is a principle that guides us in our decision making process. A value must be chosen freely among alternatives, after due deliberation. We must be ready to defend it with others and to have it reflected in our behavior.

As we go through the process of defining what it is that drives us, we will realize that there are two different types of values:

"There is a big difference between running away from something and running after something.

The latter puts you in charge!"

\- Unknown

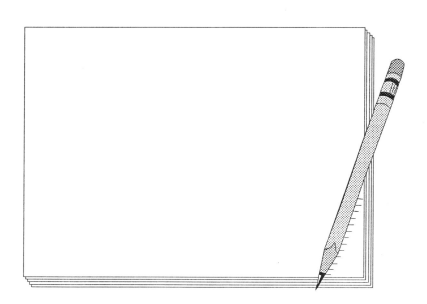

Toward Values >>>

A Toward value is one that we wish to fulfill. It can be found by reflecting on the following:

What is most important in my life?

Think of a value that you unconditionally live by.

Think of an emotional state that is extremely important for you to experience.

Examples of Toward values:
Love, Loyalty, Friendship, Family, Freedom, Security, Career, Acceptance

<<< Away-from values

An Away-from value is something we wish to avoid. Consider the following:

I would do anything to avoid feeling…!

Think of the worst possible emotional state you could be in… How far would you go to avoid feeling that emotion?

A good example is someone whose primary away-from value would be loneliness. In order to avoid feeling lonely, he or she often chooses to remain in an unhappy relationship, terrified at the thought of being alone.

"Security is mostly a superstition.

It does not exist in nature, nor do the children of men as a whole experience it.

Avoiding danger is not safer in the long run than outright exposure.

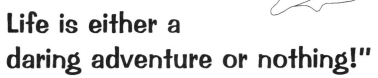

Life is either a daring adventure or nothing!"

- Helen Keller

Financial insecurity is another away-from value. Would a person who is afraid to feel insecure financially leave a stable, perhaps boring job to start a business? He or she may threaten to quit for years but there will always be a reason why it is not the "right time."

Value clarification doesn't necessarily mean that people should leave their relationship or their job. It means that they should understand why they behave as they do and stop beating themselves over the head for their seeming reluctance to make a desirable change.

In the next exercise, we will not only identify the emotional states that drive our decisions, we will also place them in order of importance. If two very important values are in conflict, which one takes precedence?

For example, you might equally value honesty and providing for your family. What if you have no food, no money and your children are hungry, would honesty remain so important? Determining which values you cherish most is a key factor to achieving happiness and reaching effective decisions.

Think back to a time when you encountered difficulty making an important decision -- perhaps you remain undecided about the matter -- could it be that two important values are in conflict?

The participants to our training sessions are frequently asked to perform this exercise and quite often, they look at their list and say:

"Happiness is a matter of choice.

You are allowed NOT to be happy if you want
and no one should interfere."

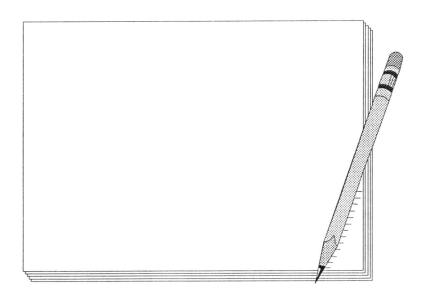

- Unknown

"The first value on my list is FAMILY, but this is not the way I live…now I understand why I feel stressed and guilty, what can I do?"

This is the next step. Now that you have clarified what priorities have been significant in your life until this moment, you may want to ask yourself what your values NEED TO BE.

What values must I possess to reach my goals and be happy?

It might just be a matter of moving some of your values around. If you decide that, starting today, you will give more importance to your health, for instance, you need to redo your list with this priority in mind.

This exercise can have a major impact on your life. Keep your list close by at all times. Make a commitment to yourself to respect your list. Refer to it when you need to make a decision. Guide your significant other, your children or business partners through this exercise and share your thoughts with them.

It would be so easy to go through life if people had a sticker on their forehead saying: "My #1 value is…" In this often ambiguous world, we need to ask, to discuss, to be open.

Many problems could be avoided through better communication as it is only in communicating with each other that we can understand the value system of others.

Using the examples provided in the preceding
pages, please complete the following worksheet.

Values from my past

_____
_____
_____
_____

Present "Towards" Values

_____
_____
_____
_____
_____
_____

Present "Away from" Values

_____
_____
_____
_____
_____
_____
_____

So let's get to work on YOUR values. Please use the opposite page to answer the following questions.

Your Values from the past.

What are the values from my childhood?
What did my parents consider most important?
What did they advise me to avoid?

Your present "Toward" values.

Make a list of your most important Toward values.

Now, take a moment to reflect on them and place them in order, number one being the most important for you.

Your present "Away-from" values.

Make a list of your most important away-from values.

Rank them in order of importance, number one being the condition you would try to avoid at all cost.

Your most important values.

Choose among the two previous lists and write down your top five values, in order of importance, including both away-from and toward.

My most important values.

1> _____

   2> _____

      3> _____

         4> _____

            5> _____

Reflection on past utilization of Values:

Important decision #1: _____

Conflicting Values   **Driving Values**

_____   _____

_____   _____

_____   _____

Important decision #2: _____

Conflicting Values   **Driving Values**

_____   _____

_____   _____

_____   _____

Past utilization of values

Now, go back in your mind to important decisions you have made in your life. What values were driving these decisions? Was there a value conflict that held you back? Which values were conflicting?

How your values changed over time.

On the next page, you will find a graphic that represents a "timeline" from age 10 to your present age. Personalize this graphic by assigning increments to the scale under the line. For instance, if you are 40, you might want to assign an increment of 5 to each mark so you would end up with 10,15,20,25, etc., up to 40. If you are 75, you will have to choose another scale.

For each of the following questions, write down the answer sideways / **vertically on top of the line at the proper age**.

Looking back at the timeline of your life, what was your greatest accomplishment? What fills you with pride, even to this day.

What was your biggest mistake? What haunts you to this day?

What was the strongest stand you have taken? What motivated your commitment?

What was the greatest risk you have taken? What prompted you to leave your comfort zone?

What is the most hurtful thing someone did to you?

40

Your "timeline"

- -
10   **now**

Identify an event that caused a sharp change in direction for you. It either put you back "on the right track" or a dramatically different one. Examples: Becoming a parent, Illness, Losing a job, Meeting a role model, Death of a loved one, Quitting school or the Break-up of a relationship.

Now that you have answered all these questions, go over each event in your mind and reflect on which value(s) drove each event.

Write them down **sideways under the line for each event** written over the line.

You have now created a timeline of events supported by driving values demonstrating how you made decisions in the past. Do you see any patterns? Let me give you an example. One of my greatest accomplishments has been writing this book with Michèle. The value that supported my decision to write has been my need to share with others and contribute. After I did this exercise, I also realized that the same value was key in my most hurtful experience. I once offered support and a roof to a very close relative. Everything was fine until I ran into financial difficulties and could no longer support her. She turned against me, and I felt tremendous hurt and betrayal. Looking back at the events of my life, and my value system, I realize that I am very consistent in my approaches to decision making, yet my desire to share and assist others also makes me vulnerable to being hurt.

Until today, my Values played an important role in my life. They made me avoid ....

_____

_____

_____

_____

_____

_____

_____

_____

... and they made me succeed in ....

_____

_____

_____

_____

_____

_____

_____

_____

What values have you been living by throughout your life? Compare the values that have guided your life with the five on your list you perceived as most important. If those on your list correspond with those that have supported your past decisions, you might feel very secure that you live by your core values. If you see tremendous disparity, you might, like many of us, realize that some major event has altered your value system. Or you gain insight as to why your actions at time fall short of your values. Take some time to reflect on this exercise. Values change over time. When you had young children, for instance, providing for them may have been foremost in your mind. Once your children left home, perhaps you began to value freedom and discovery more highly and fulfilled a need to travel. Perhaps you returned to school to complete the degree you could not complete before, driven by the need for knowledge and education. While our fundamental values are rarely abandoned, they do shift in priority over time, and it is important to be aware of how these changes mold the essential decisions of our lives.

What would you be doing today, if you were absolutely sure you could not fail?

_____
_____
_____
_____
_____
_____
_____

BELIEFS

Whether or not you believe you can succeed, you are right. If you believe you are destined for greatness, you will draw on your internal resources to establish a pathway to your goal. You will be a very difficult person to stop. If, on the other hand, you believe that whatever dream you envision for your life is doomed to failure, you will prove yourself right. That nagging internal voice will take over. You will discover all sorts of justifications for abandoning your goal and ultimately defeat your own intentions.

We have all experienced success and we love the feeling. We have all experienced failure which is hard for us to accept. But look at it this way: If we believe that failure is the best way to learn and that learning is part of life, our reaction to failure will change. Nobody enjoys disappointment and vanished dreams, but we can embark on new challenges fortified with the feedback of our past experiences.

**The fear of failure is the most important factor in
keeping people from reaching their dreams.**

You do not believe this? Answer the question on the opposite page.

If you answered honestly that you would be doing exactly what you are now, GREAT. You have achieved happiness and congruence. There is nothing wrong with being satisfied with our lives, although most of us find that is not the case.

"The best thing about the
future is that it
comes only one
day at a time."

- Abraham Lincoln

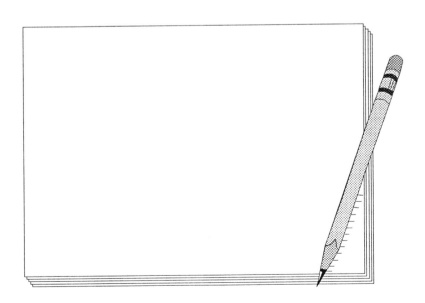

On the other hand, should your answer differ dramatically from your present life experience, you need to ask yourself: WHY?. Do personal values preclude you from achieving your goals at this time? Your values may hinder your goals, as we saw in the previous section of this book. Or do you fear failure? Be honest!

Michèle and I have worked with many large corporations and government departments as consultants and we are appalled at the number of people we met who expressed dissatisfaction with their jobs. As mentioned before, they may be struggling with a conflict in values. However, let's explore the other side of the coin, the belief system of those people.

The old vertical, stove pipe career track we baby boomers grew up with has disappeared. In that environment, you became a believer that the organization you worked for had all the answers and the best possible approach to business processes. I am a very good example of this. I worked for General Electric for many years and became convinced that its policies and procedures were the best that existed. I took very few personal risks. I must admit that the company was good in training me to take business risks on its behalf, and I did. Yet when it came to my private life, I rarely ventured beyond my safety zone. I never attempted anything unless I knew in advance that it would work.

"When a man blames others
for his failures, it's
a good idea to
credit others with
his successes."

- Howard W. Newton

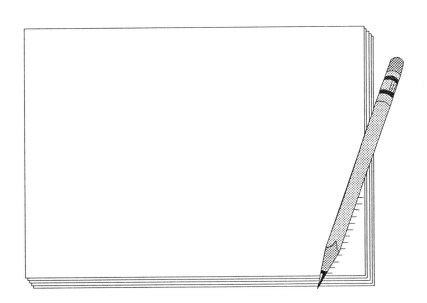

My salary and the apparent employment security created a nice comfortable cocoon from which I was apprehensive to leave. At that time I believed that the Company would assure my future. I merely had to keep my nose clean, and I would be set for life. In 1980, at age 33, I was making over $60,000 a year as a senior manager in finance. My wife stayed home with our children, who were seven and ten. We had a lovely house, two cars, what else could you want in life?

The reality is that after a few corporate mergers and excessive demands infringing on my personal time, the framework offered to me was conflicting with my values. At that time, I valued material success, but the company began downsizing. There were no more opportunities for promotion. My dream of climbing to the top had died. As a result, I had to leave. I am absolutely sure that the conditions for my departure were orchestrated to ensure that I would leave as I, along with hundreds of others, was becoming excess baggage for the new venture.

My belief system shattered. I did not believe I possessed any value on the job market. I was scared, and so was my family. I scrambled to find another "job," anything to put food on the table. I had not accumulated much in savings, believing the company would always be there to take care of me. I had to "make a living" and my belief about making a living was to get into another job using my particular skills for the highest possible salary. With this belief, what do you think happened? You're right if you think I got another similar job. I ended up working for Bausch & Lomb as a vice-president in Finance, another big company which, in the long run, treated me exactly as I was treated at GE.

"There is nothing either good or bad, but thinking makes it so."

- William Shakespeare

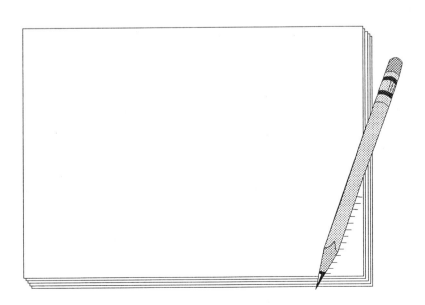

By this time, my tolerance for excessive corporate demands had lessened. It took me only one year to realize I should get out of there.

This time, however, I was not so scared. I believed that I was worth more money and deserved more respect. I stood up for myself. As a result, I became a consultant with Ernst & Whinney. Yes, another big firm. However, I had a plan. I wanted to get all the training I could to go out on my own later. I did and I truly enjoy my work.

You most likely have your own cliché beliefs handed down from your parents or ingrained in you through experience. Here are a few that we hear over and over in our seminars:

> Money doesn't grow on trees
> Love never lasts.
> I'm lousy at public speaking.
> There's never enough time.
> I am not as bright as them.
> I cannot succeed without a university degree.
> You are married for life, better get used to it.
> It takes money to make money.
> "They" know what to do and I don't.
> You have to be rich to be happy.
> Better stick to a good job than look for something that is uncertain and risky.

How would you like to spend your life with these beliefs constantly intruding in your thoughts? Or would you prefer another set of beliefs, such as these:

52

Beliefs inventory

Take a few minutes to write down your beliefs about the following topics. Example:

Health: I believe that health is my most precious resource

> >

Life: _____

Honesty: _____

Trust: _____

Love: _____

Health: _____

Money: _____

Career: _____

Family: _____

Retirement: _____

Age: _____

Technology: _____

Home: _____

Friends: _____

Security: _____

Whatever the outcome, I will learn something.
If it cannot be done with money it can be facilitated some other way.
I can have anything I want, not everything I want.
Failure is an unexpected result, but it is a result.
Living to work is not an alternative, working to live is part of life.
Making a living does not have to be hard and unpleasant.
Money is a just reward for doing something you like
Do what you like and you will succeed.

This is basically the switch that Michèle and I have made. We got rid of the first group and decided to model our life on the second.

Enough about us, let's talk about you.

What are some of your beliefs? Take a few minutes to fill-in the worksheet on the opposite page.

Which of your beliefs are expressed in a positive and achievable form? For example: "I believe that technology makes my life easier" is very different from: "I believe that technology changes too quickly and it makes my life difficult."

Take a few more minutes to circle the topics (the printed word at the beginning of each line) that are "positive" and "X" out those that are negative and cause you hardship.

Beliefs inventory

>>>>>>>>>>>>>>>>>>>>>>>>>>

Empowering	*Limiting*
_____	_____
_____	_____
_____	_____
_____	_____
_____	_____
_____	_____

Now, cross out the Limiting Beliefs one by one and rewrite them in the left hand column below.

Then, write a challenging statement for each of them.

_____	_____
_____	_____
_____	_____
_____	_____
_____	_____
_____	_____

What can you observe when you compare the two groups?

Generally, you will notice that those circled are "empowering beliefs", they are likely the guiding principles of your life and career. They helped you to succeed in specific areas.

You will also notice that those you crossed out are "limiting beliefs" and that they create all kinds of trouble, hindrances and barriers to success. If you are thinking that this is pretty close to the "values" exercise you did before, you are right. Beliefs, however, are not ranked, and they are frequently fluid. They can exist simultaneously and alter according to our perceptions. Let's continue as we have to dig for ways to change our limiting beliefs to provide us with the tools we need to be good at "Learning@living."

As you probably know, the brain is a fascinating and powerful instrument of which we use only a very limited part. This book is not about explaining the functioning of the brain. It is about learning to use its power when needed. The good news is that you do not need to know how the brain operates to use it, any more than you need a degree in mechanical engineering to drive a car. To accelerate, just put your foot on the gas and you'll move forward.

On the opposite page, use the left column to write all the items you circled on the previous exercise. In the right column, list topics for items you "Xed" out. Do not worry about ranking, it is not important.

"They can
because they
think they can."
    - Virgil

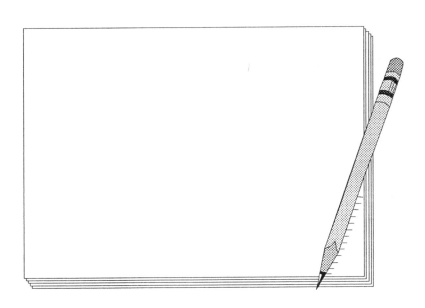

We left more space than needed in case you would like to add your own list to the one provided. You can make your own worksheet if you need more space or you can download the beliefs worksheets.

The final step is to come up with a challenging statement for all your limiting beliefs. If we take the example of technology above: "I believe that technology changes too quickly and it makes my life difficult," one way of re-writing this would be: "I believe that technology changes so quickly that I must be on my toes to keep up" or "I believe that technology changes so quickly that it is a real challenge to keep up" or, even better, "I believe that if technology changes faster, it will get to a point where it will become much easier to use."

For having facilitated that exercise in hundreds of seminars, we know that you probably think "How will this get rid of my limiting beliefs?" You first have to abandon the limiting belief that **you must understand how something works for something to work for you.** You will be amazed at the results.

In case you still have doubts, before you flick a light switch on the next time, we would like you to explain in details what causes the bulb to illuminate. Yes, write down the source and physical characteristics of electricity. If you do not have the answer, **stay in the dark.**

Your beliefs are the key to your power to take control of your own life. If you believe in yourself, there is nothing you cannot do.

"The idea is there
locked inside.
All you have to do
is to remove
the excess stone."

- Michelangelo

SETTING COMPELLING GOALS

The most common answer we get when we ask people what they want is: "I don't know..." or "I just know I can't go on like this anymore."

Because we care about people and we meet so many in our consultations, seminars and courses, we ultimately end up doing one-on-one counseling. Our training in Neuro Linguistic Programming (NLP) -- a method of managing the link between our thinking process, emotional state and physiology -- provides us with the necessary tools and techniques. Often, we help people on the brink of a new way of living brought about by a major event in their personal life or in their career. They stand at a crossroad with only a vague idea of which direction they want to take, and thus they procrastinate. They know where they'd like to wind up, but have no clue about the most efficient way to reach their destination. In this chapter, we offer what we believe is the greatest tool for reaching an outcome.

We first learned about the power of goal-setting during our NLP Certification many years ago. We knew what we wanted out of life, but our strategy lacked focus and details. On a flight back home to Canada from Colorado, we developed our outcomes, setting specific goals and timelines. We agreed that we would be very satisfied if we reached our outcomes in five years.

60

Here is an excerpt of our original outcomes written on the flight back from Colorado.

Emotional : Even better relationship between us
Feeling and being closer to our parents

Physical: Fit, running, skiing and diving
Maintain weight and "Fit for life"
Regular medical check-ups with outstanding
results for our age

Intellectual: Become NLP Masters and Trainers
Reserve one month each year to research
and personal development

Social: We attract "real" friends with our ability
to help them in reaching their outcomes

Professional: We are in high demand by Corporations and
Governments around the world
We write books and training programs which
we deliver internationally
We are invited to speak to people going
through change everywhere in the world

Financial: We have a home or condo in the Caribbean
We live on the West Coast in a log-home
We are surrounded with technology and toys
We have enough money to support our
lifestyle which means $xxx.......

... OK the "log-home" took a little more time...

Actually, we resisted the process somewhat at the time. We worried that it would take longer to achieve our goals and that we were setting ourselves up for disappointment. We got back home, put the piece of paper away and went on with our lives.

One year later, we took the paper out and realized that EVERYTHING we had set out to accomplish in five years had already happened. Unconsciously, we had made all the right moves that brought us to our goal. The plan had been imprinted in our brains, and we had followed it.

We strongly suggest that you look at your plan more than once a year. Keep it somewhere where you can see it every day, to verify that you are on the right course and that you keep up with your schedule.

We know that people are generally skeptical when we say that you MUST establish clear, precise and compelling goals for yourself if you want to succeed in life. So, let us give you an analogy that is a common experience for all of us.

Remember a time when you were driving to a new place. Perhaps a friend gave you directions to get to her summer place in the back country and you had never been there before. Remember how long this trip seemed? At one point, you probably thought that you would never reach your destination. What kind of directions are those, you asked yourself.

"My Goals:"

_____

_____

_____

_____

_____

_____

_____

_____

_____

_____

_____

_____

_____

_____

_____

_____

_____

_____

_____

_____

_____

_____

_____

_____

Finally, you made it, promising yourself that you would not visit too often because this place was too far away. Then something happened and you had to go back the following week, and the following. After three or so trips, you did not notice the road anymore and time compressed.

What happened is that after the first trip, consciously or not, you established markers or milestones that became familiar and guided your journey. This raised your level of comfort and it became easier and easier. In fact, the route became so familiar that you even completed your journey and wondered who was driving because you were absorbed by other thoughts along the way. The process you are about to experience will follow an identical pathway.

We will take a cursory look at this process using goals that are not work-related, giving you another opportunity to use the process again in the chapter addressing the future of work. You will find that it becomes easier the second time around!

So, what do you want? What are your goals? On the opposite page, we left enough space for you to brainstorm EVERYTHING THAT YOU WANT. Go ahead! Just write your goals, in whatever area of your life, as they come to mind. The next step will be to organize your wish list, so don't worry about prioritizing just yet.

64

Categorizing my Goals:

_____	_____
	_____
_____	_____
	_____
_____	_____
	_____
_____	_____
	_____
_____	_____

My TOP Goal in each category:

_____	_____
_____	
_____	_____
_____	_____
_____	_____
_____	_____

My most important Goal:

```



```

After you have completed your list, divide it into categories, such as: Family, Career, Recreation, Personal Development. Most people can divide their life into four or five categories.

Now, prioritize your goals within each section, by writing a number next to each goal. Which goal rises to the top of each section? Just because a particular desire falls lower down the scale doesn't mean that it will not be accomplished, only that others take precedence for the time being.

On the opposite page, write the top goal in each category, and from these, select the single most pressing need or desire. If one of your goals is to go to Europe next summer and another is to put a new roof on your leaky house, you may have to wrestle with a conflict in values. Perhaps accomplishing both goals would strain your finances. Think about whether you value security above all, or whether you crave adventure. Nobody should judge the person who has a leaky roof. That person might be sitting at a café in Paris having the time of her life. What's wrong with that?

We will go through the process of the outcome definition using your first goal and we strongly urge you to repeat the procedure with each item on your list.

66

My # 1 Goal:

```
┌─────────────────────────────────────┐
│                                     │
│                                     │
└─────────────────────────────────────┘
```

Is my Goal SPECIFIC ?   Yes ___   No ___

If not, rewrite in a more specific way:

_____
_____
_____
_____

Is my Goal EXPRESSED POSITIVELY?

Yes ___   No ___

If not, rewrite using a positive statement:

_____
_____
_____
_____

IS YOUR GOAL SPECIFIC?

If your goal is "I want to be successful" you will need to be more specific. In what area of your life do you crave success, business or personal? Then define your goal further. Do you seek a promotion? A committed relationship? The more clearly you can state what it is you seek to accomplish, the more easily you can put yourself on the right path to making your dream come true.

Also consider the consequences of your goal. It's not sufficient to say, "I hate my job, so I want to quit." Ask yourself what benefits you would derive from quitting. You might say, "I want to leave my job in order to complete a masters degree in business."

IS YOUR GOAL EXPRESSED POSITIVELY?

"I don't want to spend so much time working" could be positively expressed by saying: "I want more time for my family." We firmly believe that whatever you focus on will materialize, that your life mirrors your consistent thoughts. So, if you focus on the negative, all your energy will flow into maintaining your unhappiness. For instance, "I do not want to live like this anymore" will keep the focus on "living like this" which is exactly what you do not want. As an example of what we mean, try this:

Take one minute exactly to look around the room and identify any item that is **green**, from plants to the curtains. How many things did you find? Write them down on the opposite page, just for fun.

"Obstacles are things you see when you don't focus on your goal."

- Unknown

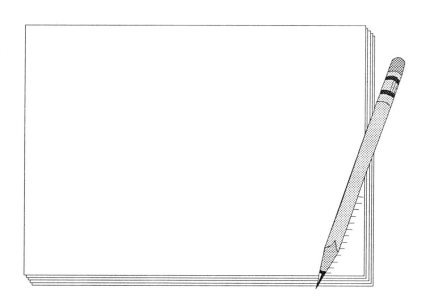

Now, we are going to ask you to remember these items with your eyes closed. Name them out loud and see how many you can recall.

Here is the difficult part. This exercise is not easy to guide on paper, but you will have fun with others when you try it with your friends.

After you read the next line, close your eyes immediately. Do not glance around the room again.

Now, name everything in your surroundings that is red.

Open your eyes and look around the room to identify the "red" things. How many did you miss when you tried with your eyes closed?

If you are like most people, the fact that you focused on green the first time blurred all other colors and your brain just blocked them. When asked to remember "red," at first you were probably caught off guard and had difficulty envisioning much of that color in the room.

This is a natural neurological process. When you instruct your brain to look for something specific, it will obey you rigorously. Sometimes, we fail to see what's right in front of us because we're so narrowly focused. So attuned are we to the **green**, we miss the red armchair and poinsettia entirely. By the same token, if you concentrate solely on what is missing from your life, you eclipse all the treasures that have been in your view all along. Focus on the positive, and your opportunities will multiply.

70

Is my Goal within MY CONTROL?

Yes ___   No ___

If not, who controls it?

_____
_____
_____

Can I influence this / these people?

_____
_____
_____

If I can't, is my Goal worth pursuing or will I just waste my time?

_____
_____
_____

How can I modify my Goal to gain control ?

_____
_____
_____

Do I have what it takes? Make a list .

_____
_____
_____

IS YOUR GOAL WITHIN YOUR CONTROL?

How will you participate in fulfilling your goal? Of course, if your goal is "I want to win the lottery," the only part you could play would be to buy a few tickets, but the outcome remains beyond your control. When a large part of fulfilling your outcome totally depends on others, you may be setting yourself up for disappointment.

DO YOU HAVE WHAT IT TAKES?

Make a list of everything you already have to facilitate your goal. Take an honest look at your natural abilities, how much time you realistically can devote to your goal, your physical health and strength, knowledge on specific subjects and prior training. Depending on the nature of your goal, these factors will be extremely important.

WHAT MORE DO YOU NEED?

Do you need to convince someone?
Do you need to make new contacts?
Do you need to get in better physical shape?
Do you need to learn something?
Do you need to find more time by shuffling your schedule?

One thing for sure. You NEED to know what you need. You would not leave on a trip without planning your route and making sure you had enough fuel to get to your destination. This journey might be the most important of your life. Is it not worth the effort?

72

What more do I need?

How will I acquire what I need?

WHAT	HOW	WHEN	WHOM

Make a very specific list, for instance, if you need to learn a new language, you will need the following:

Acquire basic Spanish skills. How?

1. By taking a course two nights a week for three months at the local college.

2. Find a Spanish friend and converse regularly

Be very specific for each step. How? When? With whom? Install deadlines and stick to them.

The "When" is also important. You remember the car trip to your friend's house? When we set goals that are too long, we get tired. You have to break them down into digestible chunks. This way, you realize and can celebrate small successes along the way. Yes, you should have a long term plan. Long term, however, is not forever. People used to plan twenty years in advance. Companies developed strategic plans five to ten years ahead. In today's world, change is so rapid that you want to be able to react to threats and opportunities.

Careers are no longer long term, as we will see in the 'Future of Work' section. Retirement does not automatically begin at age 65 anymore. Retirement may start at age 55, and people have to plan another career for the remainder of their lives. So be careful with your planning. Have a long term objective, a "vision" of your life ten years down the road but plan a "mission" for one to three years and "strategic initiatives" (immediate actions to be taken) for the next six months to a year.

74

How will reaching my Goal affect other aspects of my life?

_____
_____
_____

How will I know I have achieved my Goal?
Here's a hint.
Imagine yourself having succeeded...

Where are you?_____
_____

Who else is there?_____
_____

How do you feel?_____
_____

What do you see around you?_____
_____

What do you hear people say?_____
_____

HOW WILL REACHING THIS GOAL AFFECT OTHER ASPECTS OF YOUR LIFE?

When outlining your goals, take into consideration the goals of others who are close to you. Is there a special person with whom you plan to share your life for the foreseeable future? If so, you better consult this person. Remember, being in control is a pre-requisite, but at the same time you cannot order others to accept your goals unilaterally. This attitude destroys relationships. Include input from significant others from the start or decide to go it alone.

A great advantage of establishing goals with another person is the support that you give each other. If you ever tried to start an exercise program (for the hundredth time) you know that on days when you just don't feel like exercising, the fact that someone else is counting on you helps you stick to your goal. Very often, the other person is also down and thinks that you are counting on him or her. Either way, shared goals benefit everyone involved.

With "Learning@living," we are providing you with an opportunity to share your plan with someone else and track your progress. This is a great tool available at no cost to you through our site on the Internet.

HOW WILL YOU KNOW YOU HAVE ACHIEVED YOUR GOAL?

It is not sufficient to say, "When I have what I want." Many people set out to achieve happiness and wind up so busy, they neglect to notice when they reached their goal.

"Goals are nothing but gateways to other goals."

- Unknown

After I reach my number one Goal, my next Goal will be:

_____

_____

_____

_____

You need to set an evidence criteria for your goal, something that will flag success to allow you to celebrate your achievements. If working on a shared goal, you and a friend might plan to treat yourselves to dinner at a favorite restaurant to mark reaching the half-way point, for instance.

WHAT WILL HAPPEN AFTER YOU REACH YOUR GOAL?

A goal is not the end of the road. If you reach your objective and have nowhere else to go, you may lose interest in further development. Life is not a destination, it is a journey. We see this too often with people who have set their goals into retirement and when they finally reach that point in their lives, they feel empty and frustrated.

A good example is George Burns. Here is a man with incredible vitality, a man who defied all medical wisdom by reaching 100 years old while drinking, smoking and not exercising. George however, had a compelling goal in life. He wanted to still be performing at age 100. That was his last objective. According to friends, he started to deteriorate immediately after his 100th birthday. In an interview at that time, he said that he had reached his goal and commented that there was really nothing else to shoot for after this feat. One might argue that he lived a happy and long life and that reaching the one century mark is in itself extraordinary. True, but think of what might have happened if he had set his goal at 110!

Goals are nothing but gateways to other goals.

"Before beginning,
prepare carefully."
- Cicero

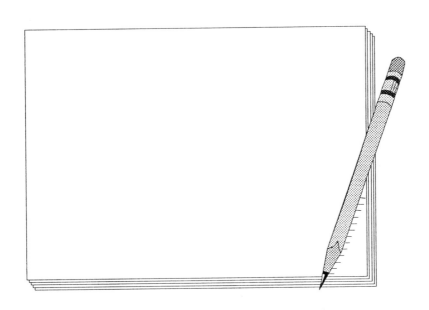

By now you should have your first compelling outcome on paper. You can do this exercise as much as you want for as many issues as you desire. Michèle and I go through the process on December 31st, every year. In many instances, writing our 12 months' outcomes allows us to make better decisions throughout the year. Give it a try.

If you wrote in this book and you need more forms, don't forget that you can access them "on-line" where you can save them as files or print them immediately.

Give copies of the forms to those closest to you. Distribute them to your children to help them clarify what they really want and use the technique when you have something to sell, an idea or a product.

Imagine how powerful your presentations will be when you can answer all these questions by preparing ahead of time. We use exactly the same approach to defining our outcomes every time we present an idea to a client. We even use the same format to prepare strategies for companies.

If you need any of these adapted questionnaires for your business, send us an E-mail.

"I don't know
what the future holds...
but I know WHO
holds MY future."

- Unknown

THE FUTURE OF WORK

Where are the jobs? We are not that old and we can remember people delivering ice to our door, elevator attendants asking us what floor we wanted and real live telephone operators who would actually talk to us.

If your job can be replaced by a machine, look for other work because your job will be replaced. Global competition does not allow companies to relax their competitive muscles. Taxpayers are less and less tolerant of large bureaucracies and demand more services for less money and lower taxes. As consumers, we expect optimal service and quality products for the best possible price but often do not get it.

Let's stop blaming society for this trend and take responsibility for something "we" are creating. Of course, if you are the individual losing his or her job, it is pretty hard to remain rational. After all, job loss is sad when it happens to others but devastating when it happens to you. Becoming depressed about losing your means of "earning@living" is quite natural. Staying depressed indefinitely is not.

By the way, this is not an "old folks" syndrome. How many university students are completing their studies to find that the job market is not what they expected, if there is a job market at all? We were brought-up in a structured environment that basically dictated that we get our education in a particular field and specialize as much as we could to become an authority or expert in that field.

"Fear is the darkroom where negatives are developed."
- Unknown

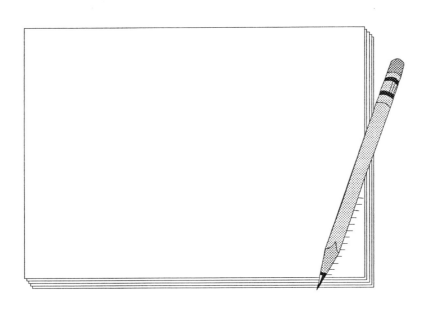

Our expertise was to provide us with opportunities to earn good money and make a good living.

You most likely know people with the right education and with undergraduate and postgraduate degrees who have not found a job in their field for years and if they were not flexible enough to adapt to a new field, are unemployed.

Specialization is killing us. If you are good at only one thing and it disappears "you're toast." **Employment is not about being employed, it is about being employable.** Making a living is not about having a job, it's about being able to afford the life you want.

Meeting thousands of people in large and small organizations, for profit, not-for-profit and governmental, we realized one pretty disturbing fact: we thought that slavery had been abolished early in the twentieth century. Unfortunately, it has not.

According to Webster, a slave is a person who is "the property of, and completely subject to, another - a person victimized by another - a person dominated by some habit" and slavery is: "the condition of a slave - total subjection to a master."

Do you recognize someone who fits that definition? Individuals all over the world have been "enslaved" by their jobs. In higher management spheres this is known as "the golden handcuffs." The salary is so good that the company has you in a corner.

"If you aren't fired with enthusiasm,

you will be fired with enthusiasm."

- Vince Lombardi

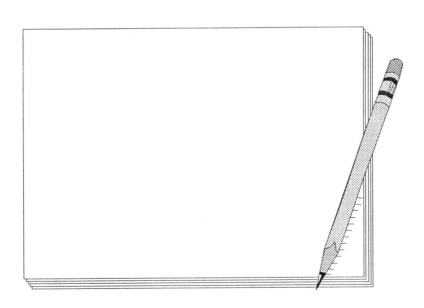

YOU created a need for that money and you are ready to accept a less than fulfilling job because of the financial return. There is a name for the profession that sells your body and soul to the highest bidder. It is the oldest in the world.

Large organizations know about these handcuffs and they may not hesitate to throw away the key. Human resources are in fact the most important resource an organization possesses. It is sometimes in their mission statement as a motherhood statement but it is reality. So, in order to keep the human potential and knowledge, they increase the pay-out to ensure you will not leave easily. Some of you will argue that wages are based on value for effort alone. Right, and Shakille O'Neal is really worth the money he makes. The reason he and other sports figures are paid unreasonable amounts of money is strictly to tie them down to a Team or a Company.

We have seen people ruining their life and never reaching their full potential because they had developed habits requiring a certain level of income and could not afford to do what they really wanted.

In Canada, we have a tremendous problem with Air Traffic Control, as there are not enough controllers to staff the required positions. Yet the existing controllers, who are expected to "certify" new recruits, are reluctant to do so, because the more controllers on the payroll, the less overtime pay for each of them. Management knows exactly what's happening; the unions know, and, of course, the controllers know.

"Those who are of the opinion that money will do everything may reasonably be expected to do everything for money."

- Lord Halifax

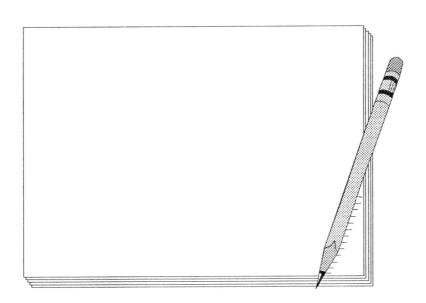

Despite the obvious absurdity of the situation, people refuse to stick their necks out in order to protect their lifestyle.

In many cases, individuals would lose their homes, because they live well over their means, counting on overtime to pay the bills. Some people call this greed. We are not sure. These individuals have been given the opportunity to make more money because of a systemic problem. They took the money and adjusted their lifestyle to that income. Who is really responsible? The employee or the organization? The fact is that it does not really matter.

What really matters is that by picking-up this book and reading it, YOU can decide to "re-learn" to earn@living. So let's take a look at the future of work.

We have researched the work of the gurus on this subject and realized that a wealth of information exists. It would take a few hundred pages just to give you a quick overview of the future job market and by the time this book is printed we would need to update these pages. We could also be totally wrong if we tried to predict the future, so we won't do it.

As this book is fully supported on the Internet, you will find all the resources we discovered as "hyperlinks" on our site. Just click here on this same page while on-line and enjoy the ride and the resources. A few things, however, we will dare to forecast.

Learn to work without supervision - Future employers will require more autonomy and willingly pay for people who need little direction.

"Always bear in mind that
your own
resolution to
succeed is more
important than any
other thing."
- Abraham Lincoln

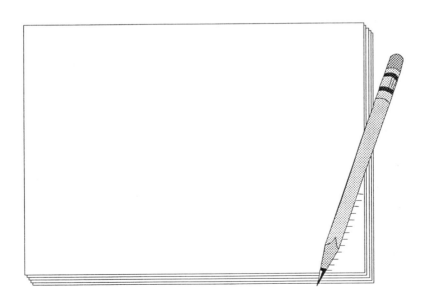

Be prepared to work in Teams - You will be part of one or many Teams that will most likely be "self-directed," that is the team determines its own work processes and sets its own goals.

Learn to accept responsibility and accountability - The time when we could blame the bad decisions on management is over. You will be part of the decision making process and will be held accountable for your actions. Of course this one doesn't win many union leaders support.

Expect that unions will change - The confrontational attitude that exists between management and unions will destroy many businesses (including government jobs) before people understand that the only way to stay in business is to work towards a common goal.

Do not expect to work in a large office - Office space is too expensive and organizations will encourage their employees to share offices and work many hours outside their building.

Expect to work from home - Re-think your house. Find a place where you can work and learn to be a self-starter, disciplining yourself to stay at a task for as long as necessary. The good news is that YOU will pick your best productive time to get the job done.

"Wisdom begins
with sacrifice of
immediate
pleasures for long
range purposes."
- Louis Finkelstein

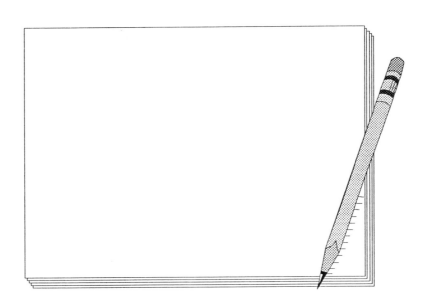

Become computer literate - Over 80% of future occupations will involve a computer, from sales clerks using a computerized cash register to baby-sitters working in a home with a computerized security system. From paying our bills by computer to making travel reservations, we will all be interfacing with these machines. Of course you can choose not to learn new technologies... it's your life after all.

Anticipate short-term employment- If someone promises you a job for life, run the other way. This person cannot be honest unless he or she is so out of touch with globalization that you would question this person's judgment under any circumstance.

Be prepared to work as a contractor - Outsourcing is a trend of the future. Yes, we know that the unions do not like this one either but outsourcing will dominate the job market of the future. You can make good money and have nice legitimate tax write-offs if you work for yourself. You will have to adopt a "client / supplier" relationship with your employer and treat him or her as a "client". That is a very different approach than the one to which you've grown accustomed.

Put attitude first, aptitude second - Employers will hire "attitude." They want people with a "can do" spirit. They will expect that people can learn the necessary skills and "aptitude" will therefore take a second place in their choice.

"Perfect
freedom is
reserved for
the man who
lives by his
own work and in that work
does what he wants to do."

- R.G. Collingwood

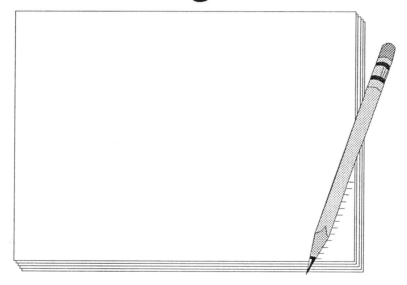

Train - Train - Train ... by yourself - Outside of specific technical training, you will be expected to take full responsibility for your personal growth and to acquire training to improve your skills. You will do this **on your own time and at your own expense**, for the costs would be prohibitive to business on a mass scale. Besides, if you take ownership for your own development, you will be free to choose the courses or seminars that interest you, not something useless the boss picked out.

We know that the whole concept of taking the reins for your own career path may seem daunting at times, but we can help you to make the right decisions along the way. So let's look at the tools you will need to become better at "Learning@living".

"Create your own future ...
or someone else will."

- Mike and Michèle

YOUR PASSPORT TO THE FUTURE

We started by helping you to assess your values and realize their importance in your decision making process. We then examined your beliefs to determine those that empower you and those which impose limits on your life. You have already started to alter your limiting beliefs by transforming them into challenges. Then, we guided you through goal-setting and we finally presented our perspective on the future of work.

We will now be using these skills to develop your "Passport to the Future."

There are very few things we can guarantee in life. The sun will rise every morning even if we can't see it and we will all die one day, or night. Taxes are similarly inevitable. Michèle and I will add one more to this list and we will absolutely, irrevocably and unconditionally guarantee the truthfulness of the following statement:

"Create your own future...or someone else will!"

If you let a company, the government or any employer take charge of your life, if you allow them to "enslave" you, it is YOUR decision and you will have to live with it. By the way, there is nothing wrong with allowing others to be in charge of your life... as long as you are happy with this arrangement.

Assuming you want to take charge of your own life, we invite you to complete the following steps with us.

List of generic values:

ACCOUNTABILITY	HONESTY
INTELLECTUAL CHALLENGE	ACHIEVEMENT
CLOSE SUPERVISION	JUSTICE
APPROVAL AND RECOGNITION	SECURITY
LEADERSHIP OPPORTUNITIES	STATUS
LIVING WHERE I WANT TO LIVE	INNOVATION
HIGH EARNINGS	ROUTINE
FAST PACE OF WORK	Competition
HAVING TO TRAVEL	AUTONOMY
DEMOCRATIC WORKPLACE	UNCERTAINTY
CULTURAL DIVERSITY	TECHNOLOGY
POWER AND AUTHORITY	WORK ALONE
TIME FOR LIFE OUTSIDE WORK	EXCITEMENT
EDUCATIONAL OPPORTUNITIES	CREATIVE THINKING
HIGH ETHICAL STANDARDS	REGULAR MEETINGS

Rank your top five values on both sides

AWAY FROM   **TOWARDS**

_____ 1 _____
_____ 2 _____
_____ 3 _____
_____ 4 _____
_____ 5 _____

Which of the two top values is most important to you?

[   ]

We suggest you write your thoughts and comments on the left pages of this book. If you prefer a worksheet, you can access them "on-line" where you can choose to save them as files or print them immediately.

Your passport to the future focuses on career, job or occupational issues and planning. In fact, everything you need to make@living. Other topics are addressed in different parts of this book.

Step 1 - Consider your Values

Now that you are familiar with "Away from" and "Toward" values, please reflect on those **values that are specifically driving your career decisions**. Using the worksheet on the opposite page, rank your top five values on both sides, those that you will do everything to avoid and those that you are striving toward. Rank your values in order of priority.

You can inspire yourself from the list on the top part of the page, remembering that we present only suggestions. We challenge you to expand on these ideas to fit your own lifestyle.

Then, in the box provided at the bottom of the worksheet, write down **your most important value** of all pertaining to your career.

Consider these skills, for example:

ADAPTING TO CHANGE PROBLEMS
ANALYZING
COACHING
ASSESSING RESOURCES
COMMUNICATION
COMPUTER LITERACY
CONCENTRATION/FOCUS
LISTENING
COORDINATING PROJECTS
RESEARCH
ENTERTAINING PEOPLE
TEACHING
DEVELOPING PROTOTYPES
DETAIL ORIENTATION
DRAWING ETHICAL LINES
DISCIPLINING FAIRLY
MEETING PEOPLE EASILY
MEETING DEADLINES
NEGOTIATING
MENTORING
PERSISTING
ORGANIZING/PLANNING
PHYSICAL STAMINA
PERSUADING
ESTABLISHING RULES
WORKING WITH NUMBERS
EXPRESSING FEELINGS
FACILITATING
INFECTIOUS ENTHUSIASM
IMAGINATION
INTERPRETING DATA
INSPIRING
MAKING DECISIONS
LEARNING NEW SKILLS
RESOLVING CONFLICTS
MANAGING CRISIS
SEEING POSSIBILITIES
SUPERVISING
WORKING WITHIN A TEAM
SELLING
PUBLIC SPEAKING

My 6 core skills:

Mastered

Need improvement

_____   _____

_____   _____

_____   _____

_____   _____

_____   _____

_____   _____

Force a choice. Which one of the two top values truly drives you? Is it a "toward" or an "away from"? For example, if your career choices are based on the desire **to avoid financial insecurity**, you need to be aware of your motivation for the job you have chosen and your degree of satisfaction with your work. You may also prize **freedom** above all, which is a "toward" value. If these are your top two, which one will become more of a driving force for you given the opportunity of being self employed -- which carries a great deal of freedom -- but no assurance of a pay check at the end of the month?

Step 2 - Celebrate your skills

You have skills for which you received specific training and others that are woven into the description of jobs you have held. You also have skills you simply developed as part of living. The latter are often the hardest to recognize and evaluate, although you most likely use these skills in your work process. You can draw on those "subconscious" skills and abilities in significant ways in the work you will be involved with in the future.

Consider the skills at the top of the page and check out those you already have and circle those you think you might need in the future.

Now write down the six skills with which you are most comfortable at this time. For instance, your typing skills are excellent and you do not have to upgrade them. Then, identify the six skills you most need to acquire or improve. For example, you need to improve your skills in public speaking. When you are done, continue with Step 3.

My DREAM JOB.....

My most important "work related" value
(from page 96)


```
┌─────────────────────────────────────────┐
│                                         │
│                                         │
└─────────────────────────────────────────┘
```

Is my DREAM JOB in sync with my most important value?

_____

_____

_____

_____

Step 3 - Your dream job

We all like to dream. This is an opportunity to let go of all our perceived limitations such as limited aptitude, money, looks, intelligence and time. Allow yourself to dream.

In order to do this, you need to clear your mind. Here is a quick way of removing all that internal clutter.. Answer the following question in your mind. Do not write it down, just answer.

What are you
not thinking about
NOW!

Now, without thinking...

Write your **DREAM JOB** in the space provided on the opposite page.

Leave it, do not erase or re-think what you just wrote. Let it sit for a while. Put the book down, go get something to drink and return.

Good. Now compare your most important value to your dream job. Are they in sync? Do they conflict?

The 6 skills I need for my DREAM JOB:

_____
_____
_____
_____
_____
_____

If they are in the list of skills you already master, (page 98) GREAT!

If not, they should be on the list of skills you need to improve.

What adjustments do I need to make to the previous lists?

_____
_____
_____
_____
_____
_____

We have a friend whose primary value was "family" and whose dream job was "forest ranger." Although not irreconcilable, his driving value and deepest dream seemed at odds with one another. For our friend, the answer lay in timing. Sometimes it is a matter of waiting. "Until my kids are old enough, I am ready to compromise," he told himself. "For now I will spend time with my children. When they're grown and on their own, then I will pursue my dream with full vigor." In the interim, our friend took courses in forestry and maintained friendships with others in the field. For him, family was the primary value, yet he was also able to validate his goal, even though it was not feasible in a short time frame.

Next, look at your skills. Considering your dream job and the activities involved, what skills must you possess to handle that particular line of work. Again, take your time to write down those skills in the space provided on the opposite page.

Now, compare them with the skills you wrote down earlier as the six main abilities in which you felt proficient. Do the lists mesh?

If not, Are the "dream job" skills included among those you identified as needing improvement?

Again, if they are not, would you want to adjust that previous list to reflect the expertise needed for your dream job?

These questions will help you define the distance between yourself and your dream job in terms of ability.

104

CREATING YOUR FUTURE

WHAT DO YOU WANT?

_____
_____
_____
_____
_____
_____

HOW WILL YOU BENEFIT FROM REALIZING YOUR GOAL?

_____
_____
_____
_____
_____
_____

If you are not quite sure of the competency requirements of your ideal job, dig a little deeper on the Internet. We have provided the links necessary for you to find this information. Then you can repeat the exercise as many times as necessary.

Step 4 - Creating your future

We will now use the Outcome Definition technique to develop a compelling plan that will allow you to create your own future.

WHAT DO YOU WANT?

Where do you want your career to go? This must be expressed in a positive way, that is, "I want" rather than "I don't want."

HOW WILL YOU BENEFIT FROM REALIZING YOUR GOAL?

To discover the real outcome, you must probe further. By answering this second question, the inner reasons related to values will surface.

106

HOW WILL YOU KNOW WHEN YOU HAVE REACHED YOUR GOAL?

_____

_____

_____

WHERE, WHEN, WITH WHOM DO YOU WANT TO ACCOMPLISH YOUR GOAL?

_____

_____

_____

HOW WILL YOUR DESIRED OUTCOME AFFECT OTHER ASPECTS OF YOUR LIFE?

_____

_____

_____

WHAT HAS STOPPED YOU FROM HAVING ATTAINED YOUR OUTCOME ALREADY?

_____

_____

_____

HOW WILL YOU KNOW WHEN YOU HAVE REACHED YOUR GOAL?

Some people might reach their objectives and pass it by. You need to establish the evidence criteria that will allow you to evaluate your level of satisfaction.

WHERE, WHEN, WITH WHOM DO YOU WANT TO ACCOMPLISH YOUR GOAL?

Where? Could this mean you need to move?
When? Immediately or when you retire?
With whom? Does your goal involve other people?

HOW WILL YOUR DESIRED OUTCOME AFFECT OTHER ASPECTS OF YOUR LIFE?

When the outcome is reached, will it infringe on other aspects of your life? Or will you feel more enriched?

WHAT HAS STOPPED YOU FROM HAVING ATTAINED YOUR OUTCOME ALREADY?

This question will serve as a reality check. What has stopped you? Have you lacked motivation? Direction? How will you deal with the possible obstacles?

108

WHAT RESOURCES DO YOU ALREADY HAVE THAT WILL CONTRIBUTE TO OBTAINING YOUR OUTCOME?

_____
_____
_____

WHAT ADDITIONAL RESOURCES DO YOU NEED IN ORDER TO REACH YOUR GOAL?

DATE   TO DO

_____   _____
_____   _____
_____   _____
_____   _____
_____   _____
_____   _____
_____   _____
_____   _____

WHAT WILL HAPPEN WHEN YOU SUCCESSFULLY REACH YOUR CAREER OUTCOME?

_____
_____
_____
_____

WHAT RESOURCES DO YOU ALREADY HAVE THAT WILL CONTRIBUTE TO REACHING YOUR OUTCOME?

At this time, consider all the skills, abilities and talents that will help you achieve your goal.

WHAT ADDITIONAL RESOURCES DO YOU NEED IN ORDER TO REACH YOUR GOAL?

This is the PLAN. Make a list and establish deadlines.
What do you need to do?
Research...training...networking...convincing...

WHAT WILL HAPPEN WHEN YOU SUCCESSFULLY REACH YOUR OUTCOME?

Will you feel rewarded? Will you rest on your laurels? What will the next step be?

Your passport to the future should be reviewed regularly, as we learn of new opportunities almost every day. If you choose to receive E-mail updates from us as we come across new information on careers and the jobs of the future, we will keep you informed. Send us an E-mail with the words "career updates" in the body of the message.

We would also like to receive your finds and opinions on the subject. Please feel free to send us your messages by electronic mail.

"Your Earning Power
will be

directly proportional to
your ability to LEARN
continuously and
relentlessly."

- Mike Bourcier

CONTINUOUS LEARNING

When you reach this point in your reading, you will have already learned a great deal about yourself. You should ask yourself this question: "How did I learn what I just learned?"

It is extremely critical that you recognize two facts: First, that you are learning every day of your life whether you do it consciously or not. Second, you MUST be aware of your own preferred learning style.

"Continuous Learning" is a term that most of you have heard in one context or another. In many corporations it became a fad, another flavor of the day. The term has been abused and used as an excuse to restructure organizations while downsizing. It left a bitter taste in the victims' mouths and rightly so. Many books have been written on the subject. In my opinion, one is really worth reading: "The Fifth Discipline - Fieldbook" by Peter Senge.

We all know that we have to learn continuously. Today's technology dictates your learning rhythm. You have learned to use a bank card (ATM), a microwave oven and a VCR without taking a course. Some of you are reading this on a computer screen or will perform some of the exercises "on-line" so you also learned to use a computer.

Yes, we endure frustrations during the trial and error phase; yet when we finally master a new skill, we wonder how we could have been so clumsy with something so easy.

"The biggest risk is
to do nothing while
the world is
changing rapidly."

- Walter B. Wreston
retired Chairman
Citicorp

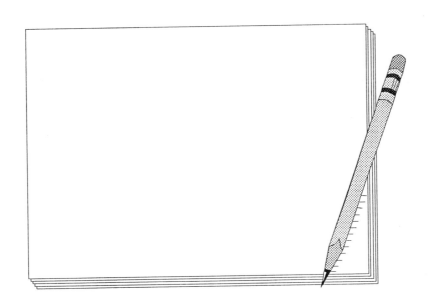

I just realized that I am typing the text of this book on a computer and I have never learned to type, at least not the way other people would like me to type. How did I do that? I am not as fast as Michèle, but the words get on the screen and on paper and then go to our editor who will understand what we want to say. I guess it doesn't really matter that I don't have the right method.

Given that you decided to "create your own future," you are aware that you have things to learn. In the previous chapter, you highlighted some areas where you felt further training and development was warranted. You have accepted that:

Continuous learning
is not an alternative, it is life

How will you learn all that you have to learn? You will need three tools:

The **energy** to go through the learning process, and that is the topic of the following section;

To be fully aware of your **learning style**; and

Enough **knowledge** to find the resources you need to develop your skills.

"Thinking is the hardest work
there is, which is the probable
reason why so few
engage in it."

- Henry Ford

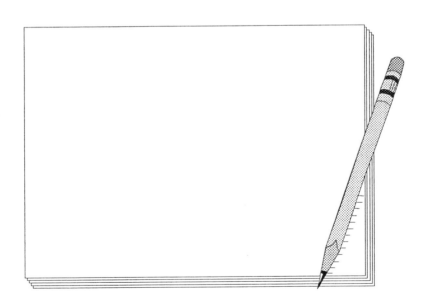

Learning styles

Learning styles could be the topic of another book. Actually, there are a lot of books on the subject and you can find them by using a <u>search engine</u> on the WWW. For those who do not wish to pursue this any further, here is a basic description of learning styles based on NLP techniques.

We rely on our five senses to experience the world and create our own reality. We also know that we are not using these senses in the same proportion. This is why one person will see a flower, admire its beauty and enjoy the experience while another will have to bend down and smell before truly enjoying the fragrance.

In a nutshell, you should know that each person has a dominant sensory system. This preference influences everything in our life. The way we make decisions, the way we communicate and the way we learn.

The five sensory experiences have been grouped into 3 systems that we call "Representational Systems" because they form the way we "represent" our reality. They are:

Visual   for images / picture / sight
Auditive   for sounds / data / reading / hearing
Kinesthetic for feelings / touch / smell / taste

We will use **V A K** as a short form in referring to these in the remainder of this section.

"Some people see things as they are, and say, Why? I dream of things that never existed and say, "Why not?"

- George Bernard Shaw

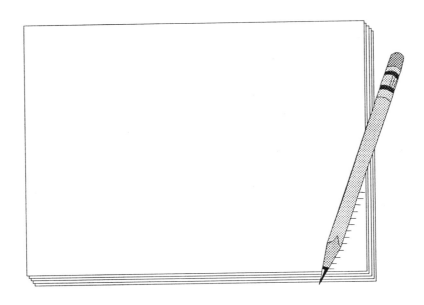

Of course these have a tremendous impact on our communication style, but for the purpose of this book, we will focus on their impact on our learning style.

Before we proceed further, however, we want to make sure you understand the importance of VAK in our lives. There is no better way to explain than by example.

If you ever bought a car, or watched someone who did, you will have observed the different strategies people use to select a vehicle.

The Visual person looks at color, the general shape of the car, the position of the instruments on the control panel. He or she will sit in the car and immediately adjust the rear view mirror to ensure that their vision is not impaired by anything while sitting in the driver seat.

The Auditive individual takes pleasure in closing the doors, hood and trunk once or twice to check the sound of quality, start the engine and notice its purr and turn on the radio to enjoy the sound system. Another characteristic of the A person is that he or she is also attracted by data. Cost is a major factor (as it is for most of us independently of our VAK preference) but statistical information such as acceleration rate, mileage consumption and number of horse power in the engine are decision making factors.

For the Kinesthetic, buying a car is a different experience. The person will sit in the driver's seat and feel the comfort (or lack of...) He or she will notice the new car smell and brush a hand on the upholstery while saying: "There is nothing like the feel of leather."

"I find television very educating. Every time somebody turns on the set I go on to another room and read a book."

- Groucho Marx

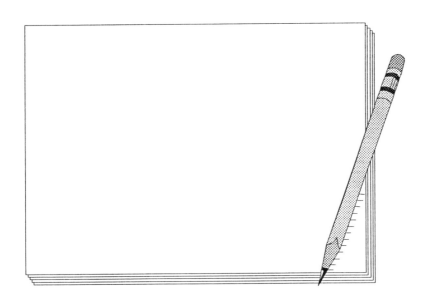

Maybe you can remember a similar experience as a couple. If you do, <u>send us an E-mail</u> of your anecdote. We like to learn.

A revealing experience is to observe a couple shopping for a car when they have a different VAK pattern. As part of our research, we have been witness to many situations like this, and we have seen many salespeople totally missing the boat and losing the sale because they just could not communicate with their prospective clients in "their" mode. If they could have identified let's say a K person, they could have scanned quickly over the data and let the person sit in the car, touch the fabric of the seat and absorb the distinctive aroma.

If it is not buying a car, it is deciding where to go on vacation or selecting wallpaper for the house. By the way, is one of the most entertaining and hilarious experiences you can observe. To use Mike and I as an example, Mike can look at a piece of wallpaper in a catalog and see the entire room in his mind. That doesn't make any sense to me as my first move is to feel the texture of the paper. Mike often asks me if I rub against the wall when I get home to feel the wallpaper. To him, touch is not a factor in the decision making process. We have a friend who immediately looks at the back of the catalog cover and analyses the price scheme and just glances over the patterns that are not in his price range. That is his decision making criterion. He also computes every square inch of wall surface excluding door frames and openings to ensure he doesn't buy an extra inch of material. He is an extreme Auditive type.

120

My favorite expressions:

_____
_____
_____
_____
_____
_____

Other people's favorite expressions:

_____	_____	_____
Name	Name	Name
_____	_____	_____
_____	_____	_____
_____	_____	_____
_____	_____	_____
_____	_____	_____
_____	_____	_____
_____	_____	_____

Pattern? (VAK)

_____   _____   _____

We use the three modes VAK every day to different degrees. Just be aware that a preference in one mode will exist in over 90% of the people on this planet. The dominance of the preference can determine the flexibility of a person to adjust to other modes, and we all have to adjust to others if we want to communicate.

You can detect people's preference in VAK if you pay attention to what they say. Normally, their words will reflect their dominant representational system. For example, here are some expressions used in the different systems:

Visual:

> "I can't see what you want"
> "I get the picture"
> "That looks right to me."

Auditive:

> "That doesn't sound right"
> "I don't understand what you're telling me"
> "Just listen to me"

Kinesthetic:

> "I don't feel good about this"
> "That stinks"
> "That experience left a bad taste in my mouth"

On the opposite page, please write some of your favorite expressions. Can you identify a pattern in **VAK**?

What are my strategies for Spelling?

_____

_____

_____

_____

How do I concentrate best?

_____

_____

_____

_____

In what environment?

_____

_____

_____

_____

What normally disturbs my concentration?

_____

_____

_____

_____

On the previous page, write down the names of three persons you know well and interact with regularly. Then, beside their names, write down one or two expressions they often use. Can you see a different pattern than yours? Is it possible that one of the persons on your list is a very good friend and that you find you have a similar speech pattern?

What about someone with whom you do not get along? Would that person have a communication mode different from yours? What does this have to do with learning? Plenty.

You learn at an accelerated rate if the learning comes from a media that is compatible to your preferred mode. Here are a few examples. We picked areas useful to learning strategies.

Spelling

Visuals see the word in their minds and just read it

> Auditives will simply hear the word internally and break it down and repeat the letters out loud.

>> Kinesthetics might have to write the word to spell it.

Concentration

Visuals are distracted by movement in their peripheral vision

> Auditives get distracted by noise

>> Kinesthetics get restless and need to move

124

How do I behave when I speak to a group?

_____
_____
_____
_____

What other "clues" do I have in my private or professional life which would indicate my preference for a given representational system?

Following instructions:

_____
_____
_____
_____

Giving "road" directions to someone:

_____
_____
_____
_____

Talking

Visuals speak very fast and use their hands to communicate.

Auditives remain calm and maintain the same rhythm with very little emotion

Kinesthetics speak slower than Visuals and with more emotions. Their movements in speech tend to remain fairly static.

Learning

Visuals prefer demonstrations, pictures, graphs and very little to read. Video delights them.

Auditives want to read all the material, they like speeches, verbal instructions and lectures.

Kinesthetics prefer direct involvement, "hands-on" experiences and interaction with people.

One final bit of evidence demonstrating this phenomenon: How do you assemble something you just bought? Michèle and I have this experience regularly, we now laugh about it but it used to be a source of frustration.

I am not Visual. I am "Super Visual" so I open the box, take a five-second look at the plan and get going. Nobody can force me to read the instructions.

Things I have learned in my life ....HOW?

_____   _____

_____   _____

_____   _____

_____   _____

_____   _____

Things I have NOT been so successful at learning ....HOW?

_____   _____

_____   _____

_____   _____

_____   _____

_____   _____

Can I see a difference in the method used in each case, successful vs unsuccessful?

What can I learn from this?

_____

_____

_____

_____

So when I am done and still have parts left over, Michèle, whom by this time has read every printed word on the manufacturer's literature, will simply tell me where I went wrong. You see, she has a good mix of K and A in her, and I accept my "A "deficiency. That's why we are an excellent team in everything we do.

Believe me, writing a book is a lot more difficult for me than it is for her. I can see everything I want to share with you but finding the words is a different game. Again, enough about us, let's talk about you.

Make a list of all the significant things you have learned in your life -- such as learning to drive, use a computer, golf -- in the left hand column of the opposite page.

Identify the method you have used to learn each of these skills, for instance, you learned to drive by reading a book or learned to golf by watching others.

Now we would like you to add to the list, one or two things you have tried to learn but did not have the success you anticipated. How did you go about it?

Can you see a difference between the successful learning and the areas where you have not done as well? Could it possibly be that the method available to you did not match your learning style?

Let's destroy a myth. Learning does not necessarily mean taking a course in a teaching institution. It means assimilating new information and developing skills through any possible means.

"Only those who will risk
going too far
   can possibly find
   out how far one
     can go."

- T.S. Eliot

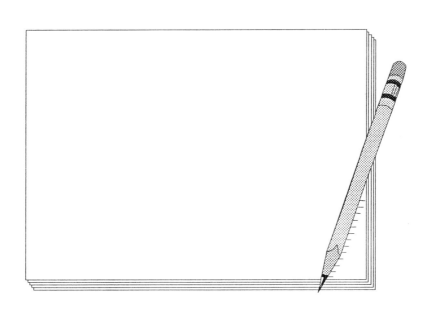

How many ways do you have to learn all the "stuff" needed for your future? Here are a few that are worth exploring.

Books

Of course, books (with illustrations for Visuals) are the first ones that comes to mind. There is a book on almost anything you want to learn. If you cannot find it, click here to access many Internet links that will provide you with the information.

Computers

What can we say? We have just developed a series of business training CDs available in five languages. There is more than games to CD-ROM. All kinds of FREE learning software is available "on-line" and more software programs hit the market every day for typing, personal growth, learning project management, learning to write books or design Internet pages. You are only limited by your imagination and the extent of your desire to learn.

Mentoring

Very few methods are more effective than mentoring. Find someone who is good at what you want to learn and ask for help. In the workplace, finding a mentor is generally easy, unless the other person feels threatened by you. Outside the workplace, I have not found anyone yet unwilling to help, given that you remain flexible and can meet his or her schedule.

"The arrogance of logic
obstructs the use
of new ideas."

- Unknown

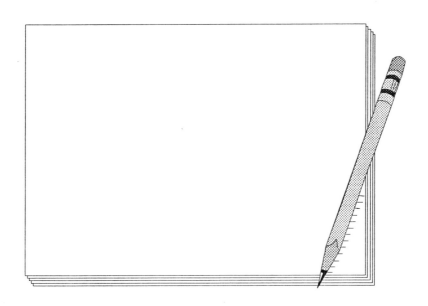

Here is another opportunity to get some mentoring at no cost while learning to use a computer.

Send us an E-mail and tell us what kind of expertise you seek, and we will hook you up with someone on the Net who could become your "Cyber-mentor." If you want to help someone the same way, let us know. You can become a mentor in your field of expertise. Do it now.

Video courses

Some video courses are expensive, but many can be rented from a local library for a very reasonable price. Use a search engine to locate one in your vicinity.

Traditional courses

Most public schools offer night classes. Use a search engine to locate the school programs in your area. Of course this means getting out of the house and this might be difficult or not financially viable for single parents. In this case we prefer the next alternative.

"On-line" courses

You can take courses, even work toward an MBA through the Internet. It doesn't matter where you live. Your situation at home or the rigidity of your schedule doesn't have to matter.

"Hold yourself responsible for
a higher standard than anyone
else expects
of you. Never
excuse yourself."

- Henry Ward Beecher

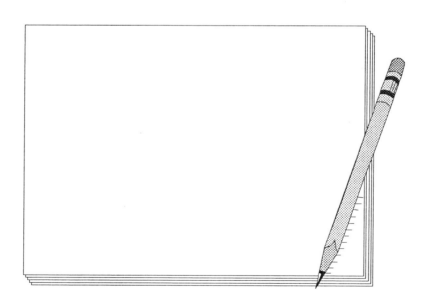

You can now take accredited courses from recognized colleges and other professional teaching institutions at a fraction of the cost of traditional courses. It is cheaper, it is better and it automatically adapts to your free time. Use a search engine to obtain more information from these institutions, in many cases, "on-line."

Volunteering

Do not under-estimate the power of volunteering. We recently became volunteers at the Vancouver Aquarium. As a scuba diver, I can assure you that what I learned at the Aquarium was second to none to college courses on marine biology. Actually, the naturalists and biologists were from the local University. Michèle even got rid of her fear of snakes in the process, just an added bonus. By the way, we found out that most of the Aquarium's permanent employees began as volunteers, yet another opportunity.

A friend of ours recently came to us and asked if we would show her how to use a word processor. We agreed, but our schedule conflicted with hers and we could not spend the quality time she needed. We suggested she volunteers some of her time at a local hospital where staff needed people to write letters for board members. Less than a month later, she had all the skills she needed.

Volunteering is a win-win situation. Furthermore, you will meet new people and make new friends. Go to your local chamber of commerce, churches, hospitals, the Red Cross and tell them that you want to learn a specific skill in return for some of your time.

What do I need to learn?

_____

_____

_____

_____

_____

_____

_____

For each of those, what is the best way

FOR ME... to learn that skill or acquire that knowledge?

_____ _____

_____ _____

_____ _____

_____ _____

_____ _____

_____ _____

_____ _____

_____ _____

You will be delighted at the welcome you will receive. Use a <u>search engine</u> to find out more about volunteer opportunities in your area.

Do not limit your search to not-for-profit organizations. Small businesses often need help and they will welcome you. Again, that might be a way to impress a future employer, if you volunteer at a business that interests you professionally. At worst, you can learn a new skill and obtain a letter of reference. What have you got to lose?

We want to hear of more innovative ways to learn. Send us an <u>E-mail</u> if you have one to share.

"There is
enormous energy to be had
from a goal if it is
your personal dream.
Yet, only small children,
fools, geniuses and
highly energetic people
give themselves permission
to dream so boldly."

- Unknown

ENERGY: THE FUEL OF SUCCESS

We are encouraging you to make major changes in the way you live, to take charge of your life, to gain control over your future.

We are telling you that you must learn something every day, challenge yourself, take risks, overlook the impossible and believe in the possible.

Many participants to our seminars come to us at break and say: "This is all very nice, but there is no way I can do most of these steps. I don't have enough time as it is now, I am so exhausted after a day's work, I could not read a single page from a book and remember anything meaningful!" Does that sound like someone you know?

To put your plan in action and really make it work, you need two things: An abundance of physical and mental energy and some "Financial Smarts" to deal with the unavoidable "money" issues. You cannot separate these two catalysts of success. They are the "fuel" you need to succeed. Their combination is powerful.

You can possess great energy, wake up every morning, jump out of bed and charge through the day. If you do not have a goal, however, you will be what we would call "dangerous."

On the other hand, you can have a great plan with a compelling outcome and may not be able to make it a reality because you can hardly get out of bed in the morning.

The most energetic person I know"

_____

What makes me choose that person?

_____
_____
_____
_____
_____

Is that person older or younger than me?

_____

In this section, we will discuss ENERGY and how to maximize it. Next, we will deal with the other component of the fuel, the "Financial Smarts."

Ready? Sit up straight and let's get started.

Think of the most energetic person you know.

Chances are that person is a child. Children have tremendous high energy. They seem to never stop, they make us dizzy if we have them around for a long time, and when you think they finally settled down, they are up and running again. How do they do it?

As part of my research for this chapter, I decided to follow two 9-year-old at play for an afternoon to figure out what it is in their attitude that allows them to sprint through each day.

I wondered if it is only a matter of age, and if some of their youthful vigor could be re-captured. How are they so different from most of us?

My conclusions, at the end of a really exciting day, were that if we re-capture the following characteristics, we will be rewarded with regaining our long lost youthful high energy.

Children ...

> believe in the impossible
> learn continuously
> take risks without the fear of failure

A memory of myself as a child:

_____

_____

_____

_____

_____

_____

_____

What specific activities was I involved in?

_____

_____

_____

How much energy did I have? Why?

_____

_____

_____

> laugh a lot and have fun
> are physically active
> are passionate
> express their emotions freely

Go back in your mind to a memory of yourself as a child (the memory that comes to mind for me is one of a summer spent camping in the mountains, by a lake) and go over the activities, the fun, the discovery that was part of your days. Write your thoughts on the opposite page for future reference.

Were you not a living portrait of the above characteristics? How was your energy level then? What happened to you?

Think of your overall life-style and work day now. How many of the above characteristics still describe you today? Does growing older require lethargy, or could we be conditioned to slow our pace, mask our emotions and steer free of risk?

Perhaps we've simply heard one of the following lines so many times, it became ingrained in our brains as fact:

> It's not time for fun, it's time to work
> Stop asking so many questions
> If you fail, they'll laugh at you
> Be serious you're not a kid anymore
> I want you to stay in that chair
> Be reasonable, see it my way
> You're too old to cry

Energy-stopping messages I have grown-up with:

_____
_____
_____
_____
_____
_____
_____

Interview record of the most energetic person I know:

_____
_____
_____
_____
_____
_____
_____
_____
_____
_____

Become attentive to energy-stopping messages from the grown-up zone and decide to disregard all but those necessary for health and safety. Actually, in order to block those unproductive thoughts, write them on the opposite page now. When you're done, cross them out. Yes, literally, take your pen and cross them or "X" them out.

Now, think of the most energetic adult that you know. Pick someone who's energy is commendable, not someone who gets on your nerves. Choose someone you'd like to model.

If I do this exercise with you, I don't have to look very far. Mike's energy is incredible, and a good example of the results of research that indicates that adults with a high energy level have retained most of the characteristics of childhood.

Is the adult you are thinking about leading a life of familiarity and security or does it include a fair amount of risk and excitement? Is this person boring or interesting? Does he or she energize you when you meet?

I will give you a task. Reserve the opposite page as a guide you will use to interview that person. Record the answers he or she will share with you and LEARN from that person's strategies.

We firmly believe that we can re-capture these energy boosters at will. We believe that we do not stop playing because we grow old, but rather, that we grow old because we stop playing.

Let's explore how.

"It's a funny thing about life; if you refuse to accept anything but the best, you very often get it."

- W. Somerset Maugham

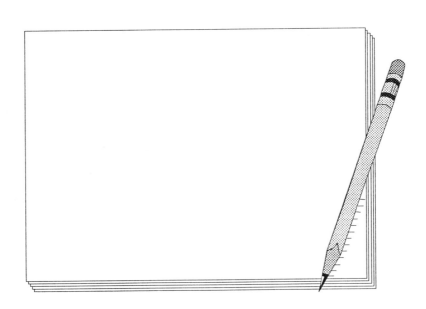

Where does our energy come from?

When was the last time you were so full of energy that you felt you could burst! What was happening in your life to cause this? Were you just sitting in your car in traffic, driving to work on a Monday morning?

Take a few minutes to think about this. What brings this surge of energy into your life?

Perhaps you were excited about something you really believed in. Something for which you felt passionate. If it was a new project of some sort, you could not wait to get started. You were ready to devote all your time to make it a top priority. You felt like sharing that project with the significant people in your life. You couldn't delay telling them about it. It might even have been something risky and the risk of failing made it even more exciting.

We believe that the safe, familiar route often kills passion and excitement. People frequently tell us they fear the unknown. We gently remind them of how they felt before a first date. You are not sure things will work out. You are not sure the attraction will be reciprocal. You are rehearsing what you will say and forget it all when the time comes to open your mouth. You might be scared of the possible rejection.

How does that make you feel? Does that drain your energy? I doubt it. Your heart rate goes up, you are very awake, your body stiffens and you smile. We experience the same kind of feelings when we apply for a job or when we present a proposal to a new client.

"An optimist may see a light where there is none, but why must the pessimist always run to blow it out?."

- Michel de Saint-Pierre

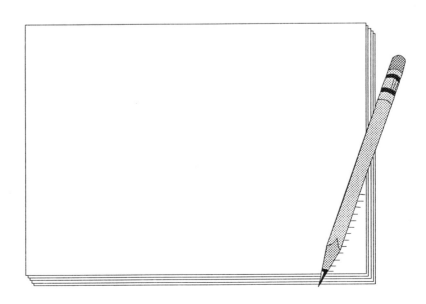

Yes, you might be scared or at least uncomfortable but you still go through with it. And if you do not succeed, you try again.

How do we lose our passion?

By deciding to live a sheltered life instead of living fully, by staying away from potential pain and disappointment by not taking risks, by not investing in dreams and goals, our passion slowly ebbs away.

We may find the safe road appropriate for a time. Perhaps, as we discovered with values, taking big financial risks when our children's education might be jeopardized would not be prudent.

What happens to us, unfortunately, is that our risk muscles atrophy into total uselessness. So, if we decide to forego financial risks for the next few years, we should make it a point to exercise our risk muscles in other areas, thus keeping the passion and excitement alive.

The best way to do that is to re-learn to dream. Including in your life daring and alluring dreams is the first step toward teaching your brain to believe in them and make them happen. For something great to manifest, you must begin with a dream.

Luckily, YOUR DREAM is already written down as you have performed all the exercises thus far. In addition, you now realize that you must keep the dream alive with passion, so all we have to do now is create and maintain the energy level to nourish the dream.

"Our bodies are our
gardens ...
our wills are
gardeners."

- William
   Shakespeare

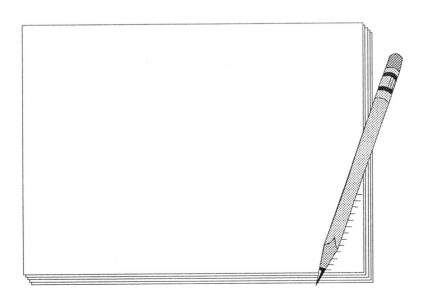

ENERGY GAIN / ENERGY DRAIN

We all go through energy gain and energy drain cycles. The winners are those who can minimize the drain and maximize the gain.

Physiological energy factors.

Eating habits are a major energy factor.

No, this is not another "diet" book. I personally do not believe in dieting. I have tried again and again and it doesn't work and I know that the last thing you need is another book telling you to diet. (By the way, isn't it funny that the word "die" is part of the word "diet") In addition, I am not a nutritionist and I cannot give advice on this subject. There are, however, a few things I can bring to your attention.

Digestion is the second most important energy drain activity that your body experiences. Sex is the first. (Depending on your sex life, digestion might be first for you...!!!) You have probably experienced the somnolent feeling following a heavy meal and depending on your activity at that time, the feeling can be more or less severe. We have attended seminars where many people "dozed-off" following lunch.

When you need to be active all day, you have to consider adapting your eating habits to your energy demand. We do not all have the same metabolism. Some of us are morning people while others are night owls. I would not attempt to give you a "boiler plate" recipe for maximizing energy. You have to decide this for yourself.

What gives me energy	What drains my energy
_____	_____
_____	_____
_____	_____
_____	_____
_____	_____
_____	_____
_____	_____
_____	_____
_____	_____

Examples:

Nature	Waiting in line
Interesting people	Routine work
A certain piece of music	Worry
Breathing deeply	Guilt
Exercise	Rainy days

* Compensate for an energy drain by linking it to an energy gain.

For instance, playing an energizing piece of music during routine work.

To help you with this process, complete the questionnaire on the opposite page. It should give you a pretty good idea of your energy cycle.

Back to food. Again, some people will digest almost anything at any time day or night. My mother is 82 and she eats hot pork roast at midnight before going to bed. I get sick just thinking about it. If her metabolism can handle a heavy meal at that hour, good for her. Eating is one of life's great pleasures.

You know what makes you feel full and what gives you energy. As long as you remain aware of how your body responds to certain foods, you can make the right decisions about what you eat. By the way, I believe that the quantity of food you eat is as important as the quality.

Another thing to consider is that when you decide to have a big lunch and know that you will have a low energy level for the following two hours, schedule your work accordingly. I would not get into an activity that requires concentration or creativity at that time. But again, this is me. Find out what works for you.

As we decided not to make this another diet book, I will stop here. Should you want more information on nutrition and eating habits, just use a search engine to query the WWW with your questions.

Physical fitness

No, this is not a book on exercise. I simply want to highlight the fact that you have more energy when you are fit.

"People who do not find time
for exercise will
have to find time
for illness."

- Old proverb

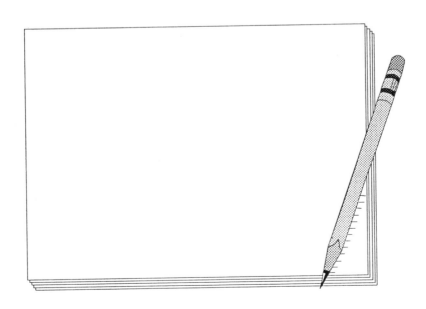

I am very tired of companies and products telling me my ideal weight. Do they know me? What if I have a heavy bone structure? If you feel OK, you're OK. That's it.

Of course, you have to understand that your hearth pumps blood to give your body the energy you need to move. If you climb a flight of stairs, let's say 20 stairs, and are totally out of breath, do you feel good about this? I know I don't. On the other hand, I do not have to be able to do high impact aerobics for 90 minutes to feel good about myself. Your choice.

You need energy to realize your goals. If you do not have any to spare, you will not succeed. Again, if you want more information on physical fitness, use a search engine to find what you need.

Body position

Here is a quick exercise that I would like you to do. Think of a very depressing time of your life. A time when you were really down. What images come to your mind? What were you hearing at that time? How did you feel? What did you think? Take one minute to "re-live" the event.

Please observe what happens to your body as you access these old feelings. What position are your shoulders? Do they slump? Is your back straight or hunched forward? Did your eyes gaze downward for an instant? How did you breathe? Deeply or shallowly?

"Take away the cause, and the effect ceases."

- Miguel De Cervantes

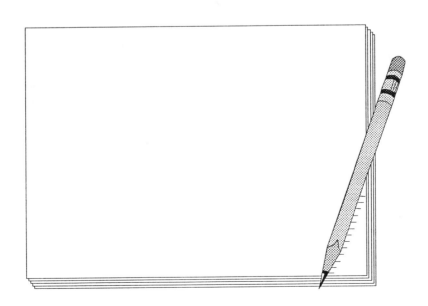

This exercise is difficult to do when you read a book, so if the process doesn't work for you, ask the same questions of your partner and observe the physiological changes in his or her body.

Now get out of this state and think of the happiest event of your life, a time when you were on cloud nine, when everything you had done came to fruition, when you felt on top of the world. What happened to your body position? To your breathing?

You already know that your body energizes you. The way you are sitting at this moment might be an energy drain or might support your need for energy for the tasks lying ahead.

When you want energy, you have to act energized. You cannot go around in life with a depressed attitude and the body to match and expect that people will take you seriously. Your goals are ahead of you and in the sky. Your head must be up to see them. If you want to move forward, you need a forward stance, not a leaning back position.

Have you ever met people with high energy who drag their feet? When you want to be positive, MOVE POSITIVE. Three more things about your physical body:

SMILE...! It is so hard to be upset when you smile. The next time you are stuck in traffic and cursing at everybody in your mind, put a smile on your face and try to stay mad. Go ahead, try it. I can guarantee you that you will not be able to stay upset.

"Keep away from people who
try to belittle your ambitions.
Small people
always do that,
but the really
great make you
feel that you
too can become great."
- Mark Twain

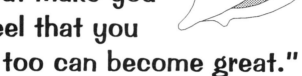

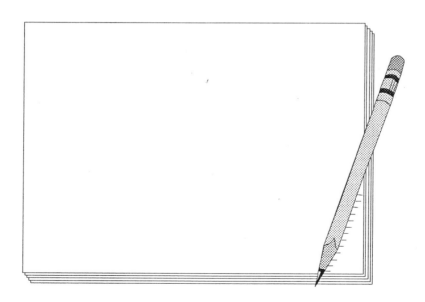

BREATHING is also underestimated. Our body takes the easiest route to continue to exist. If it could, it would hibernate all winter. We also breathe as little as we have to. To get oxygen to your brain and muscles, you need to breathe. Try breathing to really fill your lungs and exhaling to really empty them. If you do it more than five cycles, you feel dizzy. Of course, your body is not used to all this oxygen.

SLEEP is necessary to recharge your "energizer" batteries. The fact that you need eight hours of uninterrupted sleep each night is a myth. Some people get by on a lot less and are still energized.

There is a major trend in large corporations that allow people to take "power snoozes" during the day. I know it works for me. A thirty-minute snooze after lunch and I am back in top shape. Again, find your own comfort zone. The important thing is to be fully aware of what gives you energy.

The people factor

Do you know people who react negatively to anything you say or try? You spend time with them socially or in business and when they leave, you are totally drained? If you share a new project or a dream with them, thirty minutes is all they need to destroy it.

158

Energy DRAINERS   **Energy GIVERS**

_____   _____
_____   _____
_____   _____
_____   _____
_____   _____
_____   _____

How can I avoid energy DRAINERS?

_____
_____
_____
_____
_____
_____

How can I spend more time with GIVERS?

_____
_____
_____
_____
_____
_____

Let's make a list of those people in the left column of the opposite page. Think for a minute and write down their names.

In the right column, write the names of people who give you energy, those who have a positive attitude. They always encourage you, no matter how strange your ideas seem. You actually seek out their company and they seek yours. How many of those do you have? Even if you only know a few, they really count.

Why do you spend any time with the "drainers?" If they have a negative impact on you and your dreams, why bother? If you really must meet with them, here is a neat approach. Try to become a "giver" to them. If they do not accept your help, keep the conversation on them. Do not let them drag you down.

Now take the other list of people, I will call them the "givers." Talk to them, tell them they are on your list. Tell them why. Ask them what you can give them in return for the energy they give you.

Earlier, I asked you to interview a high energy person. Chances are, this person's name is on the list of "givers." That's normally how it goes. People with a lot of energy give a lot because they have the energy to do so. Model that person. Tell him or her that you want to learn from their experience and strategies. I would doubt very much that your interest would be rejected.

Use the "givers" as a fuel pump. When you run low on fuel, stop by their house or office and fill up.

What special places do I have to GAIN energy and/or recharge my "batteries?"

_____
_____
_____
_____
_____
_____

Which of my activities provide me with a boost of energy?

_____
_____
_____
_____
_____
_____

Which environmental situations / conditions should I avoid to keep a maximum amount of energy?

_____
_____
_____
_____
_____
_____

Environmental Energizers

Many environmental factors will affect your level of energy.

Do you have special places where you feel energized? Some people gather strength after a solitary walk in the forest, for others, it's a stroll on the beach. Some people become super-charged by a rock concert.

Colors can play an important role in your energy, so can music, flowers, art and humor.

Similarly, some environmental factors drain your energy. Traffic is a common one, waiting in line, routine work and boring speeches are others.

Take a minute to reflect on what works for you. Write those factors down on the opposite page to become fully aware of the positive and negative impact, they have on you. Then, it is up to you to seek or avoid them to ensure your energy is always at the required level.

Having lots of energy also means being able to relax. Sleep is not the only way to recharge your batteries. You must be able to create the environment that allows your mind and body to take a well-earned rest. This can be a 30 minute break or a few days off, whatever is needed.

"Long-Range planning
does not deal with
future decisions, but
with the future
of present decisions."

- Peter F. Drucker

FINANCIAL SMARTS

All too often we live our lives unconscious of our beliefs, our priorities, our values, and our goals. Even less often are we aware enough to be proactive and achieve our desires. Learning is something for which we all possess the capacity, but do we actually take the time and effort to carry it out? Too frequently the answer is 'no', and this becomes obvious when we think of the number of things we want to do in life and then look at what we have actually done. This certainly holds true when people are dealing with their finances. Why is that? Could it be FEAR (False Evidence Appearing Real), or is it just that we have not learned how to plan for our financial future?

This section aims at helping you to clearly define financial planning, exposing you to the tools for measuring and analyzing your current financial position, and making you aware of uncontrollable and controllable factors, as well as ensuring consistency with your values and belief system.

When dealing with finances it is important to understand that there are a number of areas that make up the whole picture. In no particular order, there is cash flow management, investment strategy, retirement planning, and contingency planning. All are independent of one other, and at the same time, interdependent.

Cashflow Tip: Your Favorite Basket

Step 1:   Obtain a medium-sized basket.

Step 2:   Put it on top of the fridge
             (or somewhere else highly visible).

Step 3:   Starting at the beginning of each
             month, put all your receipts in the
             basket.

Step 4:   At the end of the month, tally all
             your receipts.

Step 5:   Repeat for the next three months.

Step 6:   Total all your numbers for the three
             months.

Step 7:   Evaluate where you are spending
             your money.

Step 8:   Compare this number to your take-
             home income.

How are you doing?
Do you need to make some adjustments?

Managing your cash flow is simply **understanding where your income comes** from and accounting for **where the money goes**. It sounds simple, but all too often, we lose track of our income. The interesting thing is that once you have clarified your cash flow position you have taken the first step to understanding what type of person you are financially - a SAVER or a SPENDER! You find out where your money is going and how much you have left over, and we will call this your savings. This is very important because the more you understand your budget, the more you will become clear on how much you are saving and hence are able to invest.

The ability to save and the opportunity for savings determine your investment outlook. **Saving today leads to savings tomorrow**. In order to achieve your objectives, you must build an appropriate strategy based on your philosophy, your time horizon, your risk tolerance, and your responsibilities. You have to be clear on what it is that you are trying to achieve and how you plan to reach your goals.

Once you have gone beyond the human barriers, your investment strategy has to weather the environmental elements: inflation, taxes, legal changes, political uncertainty just to name a few. By definition an investment strategy should be developed to capitalize on the best possible reward given a certain amount of risk.

Even this objective cannot ultimately protect you from all the environmental factors, but it does allow you to understand them and to plan and account for them. Remember: **Plan for the best and prepare for the worst**.

When it Comes to Finances:

	Saver ▲	**Spender** ▲
Population:	5%	95%
Philosophy:	Plan & Save to Accomplish Goals	Live & Spend to Satisfy Wants
Action:	Save First	Spend First
Work Status:	Employer of Spenders	Employee of Savers
Life Status:	Independent	Dependent

To quickly recap: use your cash flow analysis to understand how much you can save, then take your savings and look to invest them. Now ask yourself why you are investing. What is important about investing to you? About 90% of people say they invest for their retirement. Like most, you will have thought this because that is what society has conditioned you to do. This is fine because one day you are going to retire (if you are not already there). The important thing you must be clear on is what retirement means for you, and how you plan to get there. What resources will you utilize?

Retirement planning has three phases:

the **accumulation** phase which is: utilizing investment strategies to create, to build, and to multiply;

the **distribution** phase which includes: accounting for all sources of capital and positioning your assets to provide you with the maximum amount of income; and

the **succession** phase during which you plan to conserve, protect and pass on any assets you have not utilized.

The accumulation phase

During the accumulation stage in life you have potentially three sources for helping to build your nest egg.

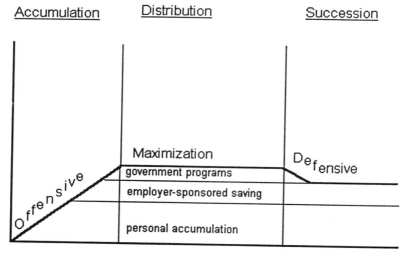

Accumulation   Distribution   Succession

$

Maximization
government programs

employer-sponsored saving

personal accumulation

Offensive

Defensive

time

The obvious one is your own **personal savings**. There may be help from your employer, and finally the government may chip in as well. As previously mentioned, you possess the ability, the resources, and the initiative to make a substantial contribution to your retirement savings objective. You just need to be proactive instead of procrastinating and you need to stay focused on your own game plan and not be swayed by tempting teasers.

The other important source is **your employer sponsored programs**. They traditionally have been pension plans that offered you the power of pooled savings based on who contributed, for how long, and how many were going to be provided an income. These offered the advantage of having your employer match your contributions, a bonus in any type of savings plan. The more recent type of programs have been employer sponsored as well but they are much like an individual saving plan. You as the employee contribute regularly into the plan but your contribution is accounted for individually as opposed to being pooled with contributions of other employees. These types of plans may also be matched by your employer.

The final possible source is the **social safety net**! If you have not noticed, I say this in a sarcastic way. Historically, these types of programs have been significant and many people have relied on them. Many still do today, despite the questionable future of government social programs to be discussed later. Suffice it to say that while it has been great to be able to collect from the government, don't count on it in the future.

Are You on Track???

Find out if your current financial program will meet your retirement expectations. The following is a list of questions that will allow you an opportunity to see where your plans are in relation to your objectives.

1. At what age do you wish to retire?
2. How many working years do you have left?
3. What is the value of your current retirement savings?
4. How much do you contribute into your retirement savings per year?
5. What long-term return do you expect to achieve on these savings?
6. What is your estimate of a long-term rate of inflation?
7. What is your current annual salary?
8. What is the rate of increase of your salary?
9. What is your income from other sources?
10. What is your effective tax rate?
11. How much income do you feel you would require in retirement?
12. For how long do you feel your income must last?

The answers to these questions are your objectives. These should be analyzed by yourself or your financial advisor to see if you are in line with your expectations or you are short of your expectations. If you are short, then what adjustments must you make?

The distribution phase

After working hard during those accumulation years, you are ready to transform your capital and generate some income. In this distribution phase you have planned well so you are going to be able to maximize your income and minimize your taxes. This consists of preparation prior to retirement and positioning once you've stopped working. To prepare, you have analyzed your assets as to where they are coming from, both tax exposed and tax deferred, and how long these assets must last. These are the hard facts. What about your lifestyle needs? Do you plan to sell the family home? Do you plan to travel? Do you expect to work part time? Yes, we cannot forget about these 'soft' but important facts. By being prepared you can position yourself to realize your objectives.

The succession phase

The succession phase is all about defending your right to your hard-earned success. You will have worked over 30 years to build it. You will have experienced the fruits of your labor for over 20 years while in retirement. Now you will be faced with the decision of possibly leaving a legacy. This position allows you to preserve what capital you do not use and to be able to pass it on. By planning for it early enough you may be able to effectively increase your estate by passing on your assets in a tax effective manner.

The final area of your finances is **contingency planning**. This can simply be defined as preparing for uncertainties that may hinder your plans and risks that may affect your progress in life.

"Contingency planning
not only accounts
for the unexpected
but also can
preserve
your dignity and
protect your
family."
- David B. Melles

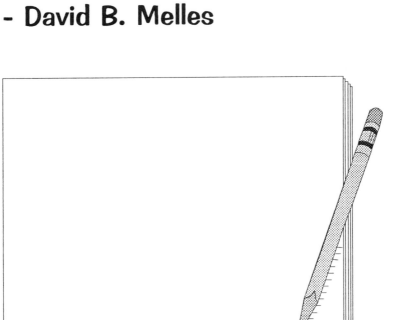

There are two fundamental risk areas financially: premature death and unfortunate accident or sickness.

All too often we focus so much on saving and investing that we lose sight of securing our number one asset and protecting the ones we love and the things we own. Disability insurance insures the number one asset anyone can ever possess in their lifetime, and that is their ability to earn@living. Why, you say? Let us think about it. If you cannot work to earn your income, you will not be able to sustain your current lifestyle, let alone save and invest for your future.

Life insurance, on the other hand, provides capital when you need it the most. It ensures that your family's future is protected by allowing the kids to continue their education, by allowing your surviving spouse to have an income to live on, and by allowing the flexibility and dignity for your family to maintain their standard of living. Proceeds from life insurance allow the immediate cash needs to be taken care of and provide capital to carry out your wishes for your family. This applies both on a personal level and on a business level. On a personal level you utilize life insurance to preserve and protect your hard earned wealth for your family (estate planning). On a business level, life insurance provides you the necessary liquidity to pass on the business to your heirs tax effectively (succession) or to possess enough liquidity and hence flexibility to sell your business when you want to.

"Your future hasn't been written yet. No one's has. Your future is whatever you make it. So make it a good one."

- Unknown

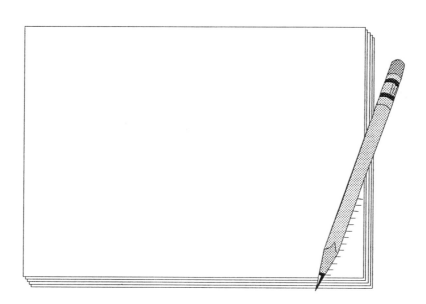

You see, your finances are very comprehensive in nature and every aspect is interrelated.

As we discussed, it starts with budgeting. This provides you the necessary measure of where you are starting from and as you evolve through your life cycle, you have the opportunity to attain the necessary resources that allow you to develop and grow. As you mature you are constantly performing regular check-ups so that you are on top of any possible obstacles and uncertainties. Keeping your focus allows you to achieve your objective at retirement. Reaching retirement is not the end of the road. Do not lose sight of passing the baton.

A Societal Perspective

Despite the obvious benefits of creating a financial plan for your household based on the components discussed in the previous section, few of us manage to do so and actually stick to it. Our real-life spending and savings patterns are hard to mold into the budget situation that seemed so logical on paper. For many this is extremely frustrating, and may even lead to feelings of guilt that we can't make it work. Eventually we give up and wish to avoid discussing or thinking about financial issues until circumstances forces us. For this reason, it is important to understand that you are not a personal failure because you haven't balanced your budget, and also that you are not alone. Instead, by looking at the barriers to your success you can begin to take control and overcome them with much less pain than you might think!

176

"If you don't know where you are going, any road will take you there."

- Unknown

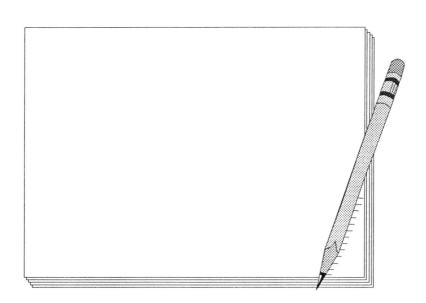

There are many factors that contribute to the challenge of making a financial plan stick. Obvious ones include emergencies of one sort or another, from health issues to loss of employment.

Later sections will discuss ways to account for these contingencies in doing your planning. In this section we will focus on the societal factors that may challenge your actual ability to save, or at least the level of discipline required. We will look at three areas: attitude, demographics, and technology.

Attitude

Attitude encompasses a wide range of factors, from the obvious to the more surprising. At the most obvious end of the spectrum are the personal beliefs that you as an individual may hold toward money. As with values, as discussed earlier in this book, your beliefs are obtained mostly early in life and may be imparted by parents, teachers, and friends, or may be acquired as a result of early experiences.

Some common personal beliefs that may negatively affect your financial planning include:

* I'm just not a good saver
* One day I will win the lottery or inherit lots of money
* I'm young; I don't need to worry about saving now
* I've got a college education; I'll always be able to
   get a good job
* My income will rise to meet my needs

"In the confrontation between
the stream and the rock,
the stream always wins . . .
not through
strength,
but through
persistence."

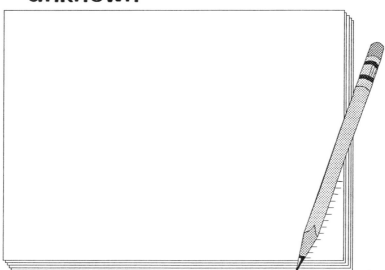

- Unknown

* *I'm just too busy right now to worry about planning*
* *The government will take care of me when I'm older*
* *It's important to keep up with the Jones'!*
* *I can't wait for my investments to grow; I need to make a lot of money quickly*

Here are some that may have helped you over the years:

* *Always pay yourself first*
* *Save 10% of everything you make each year*
* *Don't spend money you don't have*
* *Don't use credit unless you have to*
* *Never incur debt unless it's deductible*
* *Save for a rainy day; a penny saved is a penny earned*
* *Save off the top; you never miss what you never had*
* *Diversify your assets*
* *Making money takes time; start early*
* *The Jones' don't own any of that stuff anyway!*

Again you should be able to list your most prevalent beliefs about financial matters and identify the ones that hinder your success. Then, work on changing them!

There are also attitudes that become prevalent in society for various reasons, and gradually become generally accepted. These attitudes may be due to the economic climate, political unrest, or even advertising. Such attitudes are much more difficult to detect than your personal beliefs, and harder to change because of their dominance in society.

One that is growing more common, particularly with the so-called Generation X, stems from some of the economic realities that are coming to light this decade.

"The positive thinker sees
the invisible,
feels the
intangible and
achieves
the impossible."

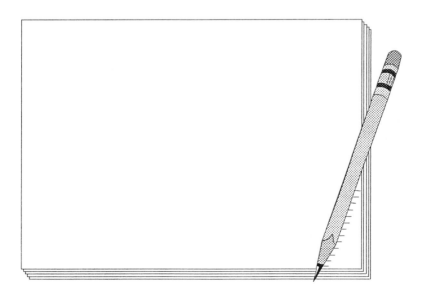

- Unknown

The questionable future of social programs, increasing national debts and associated tax levels, and corporate downsizing. The younger generation is being told that they will not be able to depend on steady employment, on governments; they will have to become more self-sufficient.

With the right attitude, each of these social transitions has a potential positive outcome and creates new opportunities for the self-motivated. Many people, however, have developed the attitude that the future is going to be miserable and there will be no way to get ahead so they might as well give up trying and make sure they enjoy life now, by spending all their money right away. This is clear evidence of a dangerous attitude that will definitely hinder future success from a financial (and any other) point of view.

Attitudes such as the one just discussed tend to gradually encompass a generation due to a great number of factors within the economic and political environment. But still other attitudes are traceable to plain and simple *marketing.* The best example that I can think of is the 'buy now - pay later' attitude.

Successful marketers have played on the natural human desire for instant gratification by making it accepted that everything will be purchased on credit. While previous generations were reluctant to purchase *anything* for which they couldn't pay cash, except possibly a house, current custom encourages people to buy whatever they want **NOW** and worry about paying at a future date.

The Hot Dog Story

A man lived by the side of the road and sold hot dogs. He was hard of hearing so he had *no radio.* He had trouble with his eyes so he read *no newspapers.* But he sold good hot dogs.

He put up a sign on the highway telling how good they were. He stood by the side of the road and cried "Buy a hot dog, Mister." And people bought. He increased his meat and bun orders. He bought a bigger stove to take care of his trade. He got his son home from college to help him.

But then something happened . . . His son said, "Father, haven't you heard the news? There's a big recession on. The unemployment situation is terrible. The energy situation is worse."

Whereupon the father thought, "Well, my son has been to college. *He reads the newspapers and he listens to the radio and he ought to know.*

So the father cut down on his meat and bun orders. Took down his advertising signs. And no longer bothered to stand on the highway to sell hot dogs. And his hot dog sales fell almost overnight.

"You're right son," the father said to the boy, "We are certainly in the middle of a great recession."

You can buy furniture and 'not pay a cent for two years!' or purchase a car with 'no money down!' You can accumulate a discount toward travel or automobiles by using your credit cards as much as possible!

Many of us are unable to withstand the draw of such wondrous temptations. Yet if we sit back and think about it, there is no sense in his kind of approach. Will you really be happy to start paying for your sofa after is has had two years of kids jumping on it, guests spilling wine on it, and pets scratching it? You're probably thinking it's time for a new one, and now suddenly you have a big monthly payment to make on something that has long ago lost its excitement. I say *big* monthly payment because the interest rate that will be assessed now has to compensate for the last two years.

You guessed right; it will be *huge!* On top of that you have responsibilities now that you didn't expect when you picked up the sofa two years ago. You decided to have another child, your company downsized and you're making less than you did then, your mortgage rate has gone up. Too bad you didn't pay for the sofa when you could have afforded it.

The car with no money down: once again, you can bet that if there's no down payment, your interest rate is going to be sky high, or you'll be paying over a much longer period. Either way, you lose out.

How about the credit cards that award you points toward the purchase of your next car or holiday?

"For every obstacle there is a solution, over, under, around or through."

- Unknown

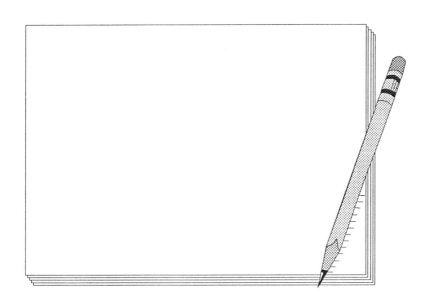

Little needs to be said here: how many of us *really* need more encouragement to utilize our credit cards? And do you really need that $50 ACME backscratcher-coffee maker-foot warmer, or were you just thinking of the fact that you would be two miles closer to you holiday in Hawaii this Christmas?

Demographics

The second area that may affect your ability to execute your financial plan is demographics. Simply put, demographics are the statistical study of the human population, its size, age, and distribution. You may wonder how this affects you, and indeed many of the effects are indirect and rather complicated. What we want to look at are the *impacts* of demographics on your particular situation, and they will be threefold: the job market, the real estate market, and retirement planning.

If you are a recent college graduate, you probably already realized that your degree alone doesn't guarantee you the job of your dreams. Readily accessible education has allowed a greater proportion of the population to obtain university degrees, and as a result has raised the educational requirements that employers are able to demand. In the past you didn't need a degree for jobs such as bank teller, airline pilot, or police officer; but in many cases you now do. This fact, combined with technological changes that are eliminating the need for people altogether in certain jobs, means that you may have to accept a lower pay than you expected, or you may have to create your own employment.

Your Financial Blueprint

Personal Factors:

* Procrastination
* Saving to Spend
* Lifestyle
* Lack of Discipline
* Disability
* Attitude
* Loss of employment

Environmental Factors:

* Taxes
* Government Policy
* Political Stability
* Inflation
* Demographics
* Economic Conditions
* Market Fluctuation

In either case, your financial expectations must reflect this fact and you must adjust your spending habits appropriately.

The second area that is impacted by demographics is the real estate market. This may affect your financial planning in two ways. Firstly, certain urban areas seem to attract more people, whether due to climate, job opportunities, or recreational activities. For example, West Coast cities seem to lure more and more people each year. This in turn creates an increasing demand for housing, which drives up real estate prices. In such places, people may pay a greater proportion of their income towards their home. This fact must then be taken into account when preparing your financial plan. You may have to compensate by cutting in other areas; but not in your savings!

Secondly, if you don't live in one of these rapidly growing urban centers, you may find that the price of your home remains relatively constant or even decreases. Remember, public favor is fickle and what may have been the most popular city to move to one decade may not be the next. Many people experienced this in several Eastern cities over the last decade or so. They had been accustomed to ever-increasing real estate markets and many people had large homes that they intended to sell at retirement and use to supplement their income once they had moved to a smaller home. Unfortunately at the time they were retiring, their homes had decreased in value, in some cases up to thirty percent.

This put a big hole in the retirement 'plan'. Wherever you live, your home is first a home, and if you happen to make money when you sell and move, great; but don't plan on it.

"Things there are no solutions to: inflation bureaucracy and dandruff."

- Malcolm Forbes

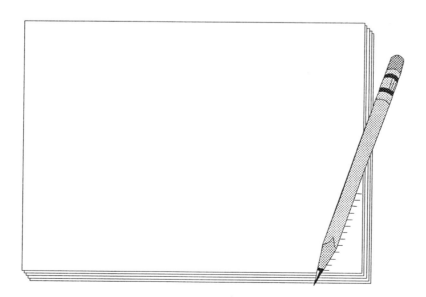

The final area that is impacted by demographics is your retirement planning. As most people are aware, the so-called baby-boomers form a bulge in the population due to abnormally high birth rates for about twenty years after World War II. This bulge has a tremendous impact on our economy and its impact will be important to you, whether you fall into that age group or are following in its wake. The boomers are now moving along toward retirement, gradually increasing the percentage of the overall population that is finished working. This portion then begins to draw on company and government pensions, income supplements, and health programs.

There is nothing wrong with that. The problem is that when these programs were designed, the demographic parameters were different in two very important ways. First, people are now living much longer past retirement age, due to improving medical technology and attitudes about health. This means that they will draw for much longer on private and public pension plans than was anticipated, and will in fact draw out much more than they contributed, including the growth on those contributions. You might say this will balance out because the next generation of workers will make up the difference, and each successive generation will thus supplement the pensions of the preceding one.

Indeed that was the intention, but this leads to the second demographic parameter that has changed.

The birth rate has not continued at the same rate that produced the boomers. So relatively fewer people are contributing to pension and health plans.

Ten Most Common Mistakes

People Make in Financial Planning

1. Buy too much on credit

2. Borrow from the wrong financial institutions, and pay more interest than they need to.

3. Don't pay off their debts as soon as possible

4. Rent housing instead of buying it

5. Don't set aside money for important expenses, like insurance or vacations

6. Don't budget at all

7. Buy on impulse instead of shopping for the best deal

8. Try to make quick investment dollars instead of slower, surer returns

9. Invest money they can't really afford

10. Don't save because they think the future will take care of itself

The problem becomes immediately apparent. Fewer people contributing and more people drawing for a longer period of time means that those who are contributing must do so at a much higher rate. Logically this means increased taxes, and social programs may have to be reduced further yet in order to be sustained. Therefore each successive generation will pay more for less. Again, this means greater discipline may be required to maintain your financial plan despite a greater bite taken by taxes.

Technology

The third area that may affect your ability to stick to your plan is changing technology, and here the effects are based on two areas: improved accessibility, and the need for staying current.

You may not have noticed because the technologies have evolved gradually, but it is much easier to spend your money these days. This is due in large part to the bank debit card, the single greatest threat ever invented for your financial planning discipline. The automated bank machine was bad enough. Remember when you used to have to figure out how much money you would need for the week and then go to the bank during working hours or on Saturday to remove that amount of cash? Then the bank machine came on the scene and you could access your money twenty-four hours a day, seven days a week. It was so handy!

But did you notice your savings account balance seemed to decrease a little faster?

"I'd rather have the company
of a janitor,
living on what
he earned last
year, than an
actor spending
what he'll earn next year."

- Will Rogers."

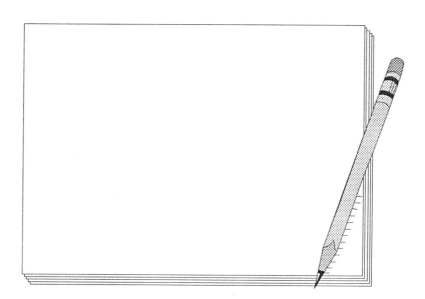

After the bank machine came the automatic debit. Now you could pay your bills without having to go to the bank or even writing a check. You could purchase things on credit and have your monthly payment taken directly from your account so you didn't even have to feel the loss. What a relief! Did your savings account balance plummet faster still?

Then, finally, came the debit card. Now you can buy just about anything you want without having to find cash, write a check, or even endure the hassle of setting up monthly withdrawals. You just hand over the magic card and *Voila!* Your purchase is complete. Does your savings account balance drop like the proverbial rock?

There is nothing wrong with utilizing these modern conveniences. In fact, when used thoughtfully, they can save you time and help **simplify your life**. But needless to say you may have to exercise more restraint than in the past in order to reach your financial goals.

The other way in which technology may challenge your budgeting is the need to stay current. Never before in history has technology changed so rapidly. The number of electronic tools and toys available seems to grow exponentially each month. Of course your personal computer was obsolete long before you figured out how to plug it in. This rapid development of technology presents us with great temptation; and it's easy to justify an upgrade because you are merely keeping current.

"There is *no* Royal Road to
anything.
That which Grows fast,
Withers as Rapidly.
That which Grows slowly,
Endures."

- J.G. Holland."

It becomes extremely important to evaluate the need before upgrading as a matter of course. For some people, their work, or simply their proficiency level with the equipment, may demand frequent upgrading. For many, however, upgrading is merely redundant. Here I speak to those of us who have never figured out how to program the VCR, and who use about a tenth of the capacity of our home computer software. Remember that electronic equipment are tools, a means to an end. The end should justify the means, even if the means is fun to play around with on your spare time!

Inherent attitudes, changing demographics, and rapidly evolving technologies all create hurdles that you must jump in order to reach your financial objectives and maintain the type of lifestyle you choose even as your working environment changes. Being aware of which hurdles are most relevant in your individual situation is the first step toward clearing them.

The Changing Environment

It has been said that the only thing that is constant is change. The theory sounds simple. But let us examine it a little closer and in doing so relate it to our dynamic and uncertain economic and social environment.

Ever since the Great Depression and the Second World War, we have realized more than a half century of progress that has encompassed high growth in the manufacturing and resource based industries. Both of these sectors traditionally depended on society's greatest asset: man himself.

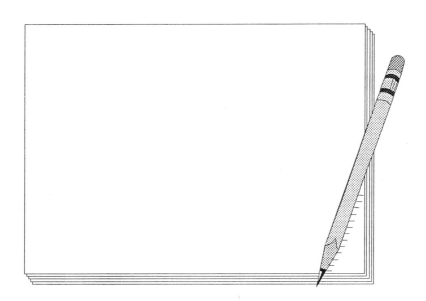

To paraphrase Winston Churchill:

"To change is good;
to change often is to strive for perfection."

Men and women went to work daily in the automobile, fishing, forestry, garment and construction industries. These were labor intensive industries. This was the life blood of our industrialized society where our goods and services were evolving to meet changing tastes and preferences. Whereas in the Depression era, life had been a matter of survival, we began focusing on getting ahead and improving our lifestyle.

Post World War II, governments had restructured and repositioned themselves. Their priority changed from international concerns to domestic development. This fact, combined with the administration needs of an increasingly complex economy, lead to an increase in civil servants, an increase in different levels of governments, and an increase in government support services. These times were characteristic of job security, low unemployment, and high growth rates.

It was clear that both the private sector and the public sector were making great strides toward economic expansion and growth.

As time progressed, large government departments and big corporations developed many layers and people could spend a lifetime gradually progressing through the hierarchy. As well, employers provided more and better benefits to their employees, and many people expected to form a life long relationship with a single employer. This resulted in a society that became content with the status quo where only a small percentage of the population were entrepreneurs.

"Restructuring
  Re-engineering
  Re-sizing...

It doesn't
matter, they all
require RE-thinking of your
future."
     - Mike Bourcier

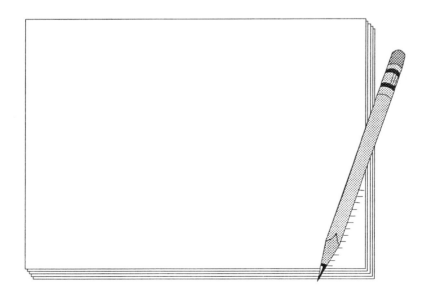

People developed a comfort zone of dependency on their employer, and this would prove a problem when the economic cycle turned downward.

With every ebb, there comes a flow, and in economics with every boom there comes a bust. Several times over the next few decades, this big economic engine would start to falter or lose its steam. Was this a general turn for the worse, or did the engine just need to regenerate itself? In fact, what began to occur was a reallocation and a transformation of resources from labor intensive to technology oriented. It was time for the computer to make an entrance and impact the economic environment. A single computer, and eventually a single microchip now had the information storage and transfer capabilities of several civil servants or corporate bureaucrats. In essence, big business and governments had over-extended themselves with excess labor and new technology was a wake up call for those who noticed.

Large corporations started to downsize and governments began instituting hiring freezes.

The word restructuring has been recycled into re-engineering, job security has been replaced by entrepreneurial spirit, employer sponsored benefits have been replaced by cost-sharing plans.

This changing environment will bring both the private and public sectors in check. People will not settle for employer dependency, people cannot afford to get stuck in a comfort zone, and people must take more ownership of their destiny.

"Who said life was fair?
It doesn't matter what
happens...
what matters is
WHAT YOU DO
with what
happens."

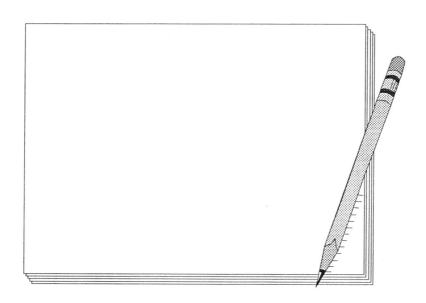

- Tony Robbins

Society is transforming from a stage where formal education was the only way to become trained to an environment where a combination of formal and informal education will determine one's success. The entrepreneurial spirit is refueling the economic environment. For example, knowledge-based industries and service-based industries are emerging and impacting as much as the traditional industries. This society is progressing, changing, and evolving quicker, more often, and with greater consequence. The economic and social environments are very dynamic and explosive. As individuals, how are we measuring up to the change, or are we even aware?

The Impact of Life Change on your Financial Picture

Let's look at some of the possible causes of life change that will affect your lifestyle, both financially and otherwise. These causes can be broken down into three main groups as follows:

* those due to *the changing economic environment*
* those due to *non-economic 'uncontrollables'*
* those that are a matter of *choice*

The Changing Environment was discussed in some detail earlier. We looked at how economic change was leading to corporate and government downsizing and necessitating more part-time, contract work, and self-employment. One likely outcome of such changes is an impact on your employment situation, whether through the loss of a salaried job, a switch to temporary contract work, or merely the loss of certain benefits previously provided by an employer.

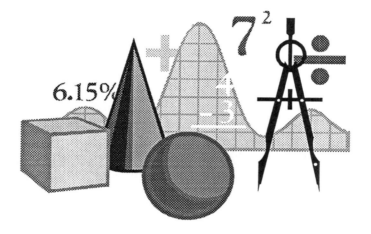

Each of these may mean an effective decrease in income, at least temporarily. They may also mean relocation or the need to create an office environment at home. At the very least, they are likely to lead to less certainty in life.

Taxes, inflation, interest rates, real estate markets, and the growth rate of different business sectors will also continue to fluctuate. These changes will impact the amount of money that ends up in your pocket at the end of the day.

Non-economic *'uncontrollables'* are those things that happen in life over which you have no control. Usually, they are unpleasant. They may include such things as death of a loved one, a disability that keeps you from working, the sudden need to provide care for elderly parents or other ailing family members, the loss of a business or marital breakdown.

On a more pleasant note, some changes you *choose* willingly. You may choose to get married, have a child, leave your job and start a business, retire early, move to a new city, go back to school, change careers, move your office into your home, or work via electronic technology from a cabin in the woods.

Measuring your Current Financial Position

The dynamic and uncertain economic environment poses many challenges. As previously mentioned, societal perspectives are changing as economic transformations take place. We see the changes happening, we hear of examples, and we sense the possible implications. How can we avoid becoming victims of this transformation?

Where are you living with respect to your means?
To Calculate your net income . . .
List all your numbers both monthly and annually:

Income Generated:	Monthly	Annually
* Employment Income	$ _____	$ _____
* Business Income	_____	_____
* Investment Income	_____	_____
* Pension Income	_____	_____
* Income from any government benefit	_____	_____
* Rental Income	_____	_____
* Other	_____	_____
A. TOTAL INCOME:	$ _____	$ _____

Less:

Taxes from. . .

	Monthly	Annually
* Personal Income	$ _____	$ _____
* Business Income	_____	_____
* Investment Income	_____	_____
* Pension Income	_____	_____
* Benefit Income	_____	_____
* Rental Income	_____	_____
* Other Income	_____	_____
B. TOTAL TAXES:	$ _____	$ _____
C. NET DISPOSABLE INCOME AFTER TAXES:	$ _____	$ _____

What mechanisms do we have at our disposal to let us know how well we are positioned with respect to our goals? Do we need to make some fundamental changes to our lifestyles or can we merely make some minor adjustments with respect to our means?

Let's look at your spending habits to get a clear picture of how you live with respect to your means. For our purposes we will define means as the after-tax dollars spent. This is the same as net disposable income, before you allocate your dollars to various financial needs and wants.

To better understand your financial position, you have to ascertain if you are

> i) living within your means
> ii) living beyond your means, or
> iii) living below your means

"Living *within* your means" is spending exactly what you make. In other words, the after tax dollars you bring in allow you to allocate them to meet all your financial needs and wants. In this case you do not have a lot of extra money to either save or spend, but nor do you rely on credit to make ends meet.

"Living *beyond* your means" is spending more than you make. In this scenario you are relying on other sources of money than what you earn to facilitate your needs and wants. Being in this position does not allow you to save because you have to borrow to live.

Now let's look at your expenses . . .

Necessities:

* Mortgage/Rent	$_____	$_____
* Property Taxes	_____	_____
* House Insurance	_____	_____
* Utilities	_____	_____
* Maintenance	_____	_____
* School Expenses	_____	_____
* Transportation	_____	_____
* Food	_____	_____
* Clothing	_____	_____
* Medical/Dental	_____	_____

Debt Servicing:

* Bank Loan	_____	_____
* Personal Loan	_____	_____
* Family Loan	_____	_____
* Credit Cards	_____	_____
* Line of Credit	_____	_____
* Other	_____	_____

Luxuries:

* Entertainment	_____	_____
* Travel	_____	_____
* Club Membership(s)	_____	_____
* Boat	_____	_____
* Camper/R.V.	_____	_____

D. **TOTAL EXPENSES:** $_____ $_____

"Living *below* your means" is spending less than you make. This is a situation where you can find yourself having extra money left over after you have met your responsibilities and you may allocate some money toward savings.

Now let us look at the measuring tool that allows you to see how you have positioned yourself. First of all, take an account of your net disposable income from all sources, both earned and unearned. Then take a full account of where all your money goes. You can categorize your spending into four main categories: necessities, luxuries, waste and savings.

Necessities are your rent or mortgage, phone, food, clothing etc., essentially your basic needs.

Luxuries are things such as dining out, movies, trips or skiing. You do not **need** luxuries, but they certainly make life more enjoyable.

Waste can be defined as "I do not know where it went" money. Sound familiar? These are dollars spent not all at once but in drips and drabs on little things that you did not necessarily want or need. The money disappears slowly over time without your realizing it.

The last category is savings. If you have a program set up allocating money toward savings, you categorize it under your necessities.

When you tally your totals, do not forget your debt servicing. By this I mean you could have loans, credit card payments, or a mortgage.

Finally, we'll calculate your position relative to your means:

TOTAL INCOME -   TOTAL EXPENSES   =   SURPLUS/(DEFICIT)

(C)   - (D)   =(E)

If E is positive, congratulations; you are spending less than you make, or living *below* your means. In this case you are able to save something each month or year.

If E is zero, you are spending exactly what you make or living *within* your means. In this case you are not going into debt, but you are not saving anything either.

If E is negative, you are spending more than you make, or living *beyond* your means. Not only do you have nothing left to save, but you must rely on borrowing to make ends meet each month or year.

To look further at your total liabilities (mortgage payments not included), you can see which debts should be cleared and which debts you need to incur.

If you have a balance that is beyond your ability to pay and have to service it over a period of time, you have extended yourself beyond your means.

If your debt-to-income ratio is manageable and you have a schedule to pay it off in the short run, then that debt can be seen as living within your means.

If you do not have any unmanageable debt, then you live below your means. The key to this exercise is that you are not spending more than you are earning or are able to earn.

Regular financial checkups help you understand your current position in relation to your income and objectives. As you progress through your life cycle, you are going to make decisions that may or may not be prudent.

Living in an uncertain society does not help. But if you have a game plan, you can make the necessary adjustments to allow you to stay on course. If you are not prepared, then you can become a victim of the economic realities. Do you really want to experience that?

No matter what causes your life change, whether it is positive or challenging, the change must be dealt with emotionally and logistically, but also financially. What follows is a look at three hypothetical families. These examples will illustrate how various types of life change affect people in each situation.

"Take the waste out of
your spending;

you'll drive the
haste out of
your life."

- J.P. Morgan

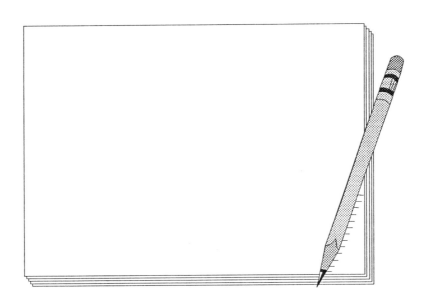

I. Paul & Nancy Jones; live beyond their means

Paul and Nancy have been married three years. Paul works in a management position with the government and makes $45,000 a year. Nancy is a geologist making the same amount working for a private mining company. The mining company pays well but offers no other benefits, so both are on Paul's plan for health care, dental care, long-term disability, and life insurance. Between them they gross $90,000, but they do not live frugally. It actually costs them $100,000 to live, including taxes. They recently bought a fancy two-bedroom condo in the West Coast city where they live and they have a large mortgage payment. Each year they travel east to visit her parents in the summer, and then each Christmas they go somewhere tropical for a couple of weeks.

They each have a brand new car; Nancy's is leased and Paul's was purchased at a 'no money down' sale and they are now making payments on it. They have no children but plan in two years for Nancy to stop working temporarily and have a child, they hope the first of two. They have no savings and have done little financial planning because they realize they will have to start planning more carefully once they have a child. In the meantime, they want to enjoy themselves.

For the last couple of years they have relied on a large line of credit and on credit cards to make up the shortfall each year.

"A bend in the road is not the end of the road...

unless you fail to make the turn."

- Unknown

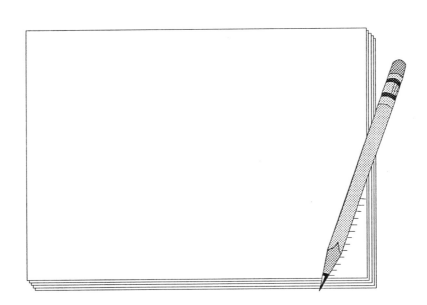

Life Change #1: environmental

Paul and Nancy live the high life and are the envy of all their friends, until one Friday afternoon in March when Paul gets his layoff news. His department was being integrated with another and although he has always done a good job, he is simply redundant now. He is to work until the end of the month and then will receive a small settlement to carry him over until he finds new employment.

The news shocks Paul and Nancy, but they are confident that he will get a new job quickly because of his experience in middle-management. Four months later they begin to worry. He has not found anything yet although he has been offered positions in the East but declined because of Nancy's job and because they don't want to move. The settlement has been used up in paying for private health and dental coverage to replace what they had through the government job and in helping them get by for the last four months. The line of credit is fully extended and all but one credit cards are maxed-out as well. This month they can't meet all their payments and something has to go. After much consideration, they decide that Paul's car should be relinquished and the equity used to purchase a second-hand car. Unfortunately when he talks to the dealer he finds out that he has very little equity; he put nothing down and the bulk of what he has been paying each month has been interest. They decide to relinquish the car anyway, but this makes Paul's job hunting difficult because Nancy uses her car for field work and they don't live near public transit.

"Few people
plan to fail;
most simply fail
to plan."

- Unknown

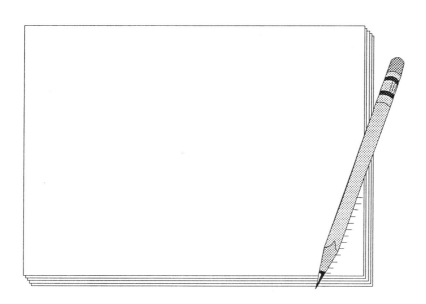

After another month, Paul finally lands a $35,000 job with a small manufacturing company, managing its sales staff. He and Nancy are happy though because he has the potential to increase his income through commission if he finds new clients for the company. The company offers no benefits and hires Paul on a one-year renewable contract. Paul and Nancy are playing catch-up now in a big way. They have had to curtail much of their social life in order to cut spending. They are paying only the minimums on their credit card payments and last month they had to cancel their trip to visit her parents in order to make the mortgage and car-lease payments. She is upset because it will be the first year they have not been able to visit her parents and Paul feels that she blames him, even though it isn't his fault that he lost his job. Their relationship shows obvious signs of stress.

Life Change #2: 'uncontrollable'

A year after Paul has been on the new job, things are going well. Paul has worked extremely hard and has managed to increase his income through commission so that he is back where he was at $45,000 for the year. He is pleased when the company renews his contract for another year and offers him a car allowance if he will become responsible for a larger territory. A small bank loan allows him to purchase a decent used car and the allowance helps him cover the payments.

Nancy spends about half of her working time in field work at mine locations and is also provided a car allowance for driving there.

216

Let's take a look at your insured assets . . .

What do you own?   **What do you pay to insure it?**

Home: Annual premium of
    Valued at $_____ $_____

Car: Annual premium of
    Valued at $_____ $_____

Personal Assets: Annual premium of
    Valued at $_____ $_____

Your Income:*   Annual premium of
    Valued at $_____ $_____ **

* Think of the total value of your income for the rest of your working life. For example, if you are currently 40 years old and making $4000 per month, your potential earnings to age 65, assuming a 5% increase each year is **$ 2,290,901!!**

** This premium is for *income protection*, or *disability* insurance.

Unfortunately, one evening on the way home from a mine she is rear-ended by a truck at high speed and injures her back. Although her back can heal with the help of physical therapy, doctors warn her that she must not go back to work for at least a year.

Her leased car was written-off and the trucker's insurance company paid out to the lease company. Nancy had no equity in the car so she gets nothing for it. The trucking company's insurance will cover the cost of Nancy's hospital stay and her physiotherapy, but will not replace her income while she is unable to work. Paul and Nancy have no disability insurance because when they were replacing the benefits from Paul's old government job, they had felt that private disability insurance was too expensive and had decided against it. Their only potential source of income is to sue the trucking company for damages, but their lawyer estimates that it will take three to four years to see any settlement from such a suit. Paul and Nancy feel that with their reduced spending, no more car lease payments, and Paul's $45,000 income, they should be able to get by for the year that she is off.

In the meantime their main concern is to rehabilitate Nancy. Once back at home, she is still very limited in the time she can spend out of bed and in her activities. She requires much care; Paul must prepare all the meals and does all the housework, which they had previously split. He must help her with exercises at home and drive her to the pool and to therapy every day. He finds that he is able to devote less time to work, but his mind is not on his job anyway because he worries about his wife.

The most likely outcome of a long-term disability is . . . divorce.

Nine out of ten long-term disabilities lead to marital breakdown.

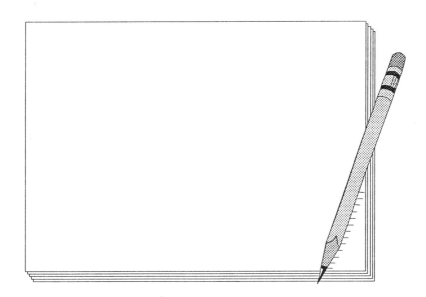

She is very determined, but the extent of the damage is worse than they had originally thought and after six months the doctors say that after a year, she will only be able to go back to work part time. The mining company has assured her that they will keep her job open if she is able to return to work after one year. They are unsure though if they will be able to provide part-time work.

The other problem that surfaces after six months is that Paul's income drops. He has been doing the minimum at work and has not opened any new accounts to produce commission. It looks like he will gross little more than his base salary for the year if things continue. They have been unable to pay anything toward their extended line of credit for some months now and the bank has decided to foreclose on it; $8,000 must be paid by the end of the following month.   There are no savings, they can't sell the one remaining car because Paul has to use it for work, and it's not worth $8,000 anyway.   Their only equity is in the condo.   They had originally decided that they would do anything to try to keep it, but the mortgage put so much pressure on Paul, that they are now almost relieved to see it go.

Life Change #3: choices

Eventually Nancy is back on her feet and able to return to the mining company where she finds part-time work.

Paul's contract has been renewed for a probationary period of six months and will not be renewed again if he cannot bring in some new accounts. They live in a rented one-bedroom apartment near Paul's office.

Smart Shoppers
Beware of Bargains in:

* **Parachutes**

* **Fire Extinguishers**

* **Life Preservers**

* **Open-heart Surgery, and**

* **Life Insurance**

It is now two years since our story began and time for Paul and Nancy to have their first child. They sit down to discuss it one evening and find that their choices now are limited. They want to start having children before it's too late, but they can't imagine trying to support a child in their current situation. They decide to wait until their debts are paid off and they are back on their feet; perhaps in another two years.

II. Dennis and Maureen Dupree; live at their means:

Dennis and Maureen are at the same income levels as the Jones's. However, they live on the $90,000 gross that they bring in each year and do not spend more than this. They have access to credit cards and a line of credit but only spend on them to the amount they can pay off each month. They live in a one-bedroom condo that they purchased a year ago and on which they are now making mortgage payments.

Dennis has an older car that he owns outright and Maureen has a new one on which they are making payments. They take one two-week vacation each year, usually to stay with her parents. They do not feel they live a lavish lifestyle but "there's never anything left over at the end of the month" and they "don't know where it all goes."

They have no savings and although they do draw up a budget each month they have no real financial plan in place and the budget is only a rough guideline for them.

"In life what sometimes
appears to be the
end is really
a new beginning."

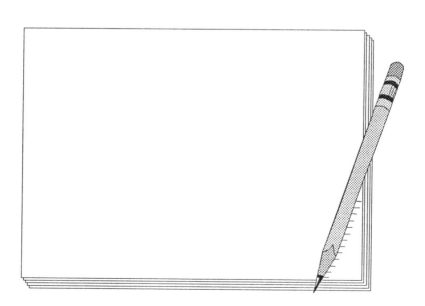

- Unknown

Life Change #1: environmental

When Dennis receives his layoff notice from the government, he and Maureen are upset but not terribly surprised because there have been rumors for some time about integrating his department with another. Dennis has been keeping an eye out for similar jobs in the private sector and has seen a few, but all would involve taking a pay cut. They discuss it, and eventually decide that he should hold out for a couple of months to look for something with a closer income to what he had been making with the government. In the meantime they can utilize their line of credit to make up the shortfall.

They decide immediately to replace all the benefits that they had received through Dennis' work: extended health and dental coverage, and life and disability insurance. They purchase each of these privately and although they now have to pay quite a bit more, it is worth the peace of mind to them. After three months, Dennis accepts a job, a one-year renewable contract with a private manufacturing firm managing their sales staff for a salary of $35,000 per year, plus commissions. If he brings in new clients this should allow him to make about $45,000, as he did before.

The line of credit and the credit cards have become fairly extended over the last three months. Dennis and Maureen draw up new budgets to cut their expenditures and embark on paying off the debt. They seem unable to meet the new budget, though, and it takes them almost a year to get rid of the debt completely.

"If you have built castles in
the air, your work
need not be lost;
that is where they
should be.
Now put foundations
under them."

-Henry David Thoreau

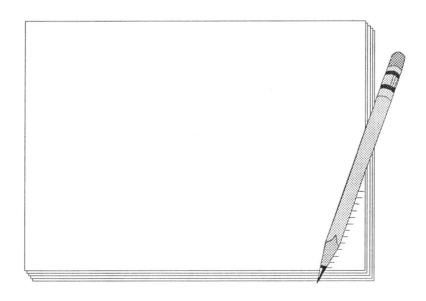

Life Change #2: uncontrollable

After Maureen's accident (same scenario as before), they only have to wait 30 days before they can begin collecting two-thirds of her income from her disability insurance policy. They both found the accident very emotionally trying and are glad at least not to have to worry about the basic income requirements while they focus on rehabilitating Maureen. The insurance money from the truck driver that hit her has gone to pay out the finance company for her car. There wasn't anything left over for Dennis and Maureen, but they no longer have to make the car payment each month. They are able to allocate part of that to cover the cost of having someone come into their home to prepare meals and help Maureen with exercises. Dennis doesn't have to leave work in the middle of the day. As Maureen won't be working again for at least a year, they look for other ways to cut costs and immediately cancel their travel plans.

Over the year Dennis' income slips a little because of his worry about his wife, but he is still able to bring in about $40,000.

With this, plus two-thirds of Maureen's income from disability, they manage to get by but still run up another big debt on their line of credit and credit cards. They are glad when after a year, Maureen is allowed to go back to work part-time. Her disability insurance policy is a good one and even though she goes back part time, it will still make up the remainder of her income. Dennis' contract is renewed and they can put their energy now into tackling the debt again.

"If you wait a
while before
making a decision,
you make a wiser
decision."

- Unknown

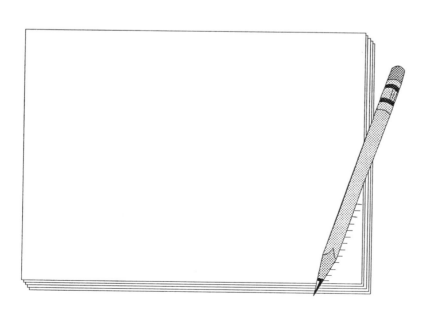

Life Change #3: choices

Dennis and Maureen had originally thought about having a child this year, and they sit down one evening to discuss it. They begin by taking stock of their situation.

Recent events have left them with quite a bit of debt to pay off. They need to find a car for Maureen, and if they had a child they would need a bigger place to live. They had wanted to be in a position where Maureen could take a year off work to be with the child, but in order to do that they would need to have saved a good amount of money for a reserve. They decide to wait a year and re-examine their situation at that time. In the meantime they decide to consult a financial planner and see if she can help them create a workable budget and actually start saving some money each month.

III. Todd and Jane Miller; live below their means:

Todd and Jane are once again in the same careers and at the same income levels as our previous two couples. The difference is that their living expenses are significantly lower than the $90,000 a year that they bring in. They have worked with a financial planner since before marrying.

They are excited about making their plan work. They have created a reserve account of three months' net income, which they keep in very liquid investments such as government bonds and a money market account. Their reserve is complemented by a line of credit which they have available but have never used.

228

"You cannot control the
winds of change...
but you can set
your sails
accordingly."

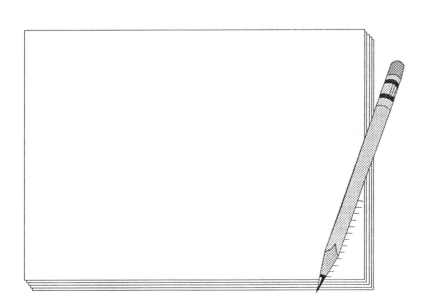

- Unknown

Each year they save ten to fifteen percent of their income for retirement and make sure that as much of this as possible is in investments that regulation allows to be tax sheltered, such as an IRA. They have personal life and disability insurance plans to complement the benefits they have through Todd's work with the government.   A year ago they bought an older house just outside the city and they fixed it up to include a separate suite downstairs that they rent out to cover their mortgage. Each has an older car that is completely paid for. They take three weeks vacation each year; every other year they go east to visit Jane's parents and on alternating years they usually do a road trip south.

Life Change #1: environmental

When Todd loses his management job with the government, he and Jane are prepared. They have been planning for some time that Todd would eventually start his own business as a management consultant. This would be a little sooner than they expected but the mortgage is taken care of and they have no other major bills, so it seems like the perfect opportunity. They use the small settlement from the government to buy a computer and some used office furniture and they turn the den into a home office.

Over the last couple of years Todd has been building an inventory of contacts, people whom he thought could one day use his services, so now he begins the process of looking for clients. He and Jane know it will be tough at first but believe the long term potential is very good.

"Choice is better than no choice."

- NLP Pre-supposition

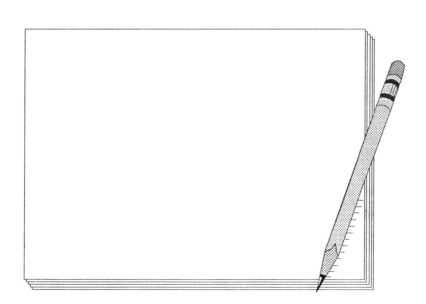

It takes two months to get his first contract and they have had to dip into the reserve fund a bit, but they are happy that business eventually picks up.

Life Change #2: uncontrollable

After the first contract, Todd obtained several more that year and ended up making $30,000. This is actually better than they expected for his first year and they celebrate by going up to a resort in the mountains to relax together for a three day weekend. Unfortunately, a couple of weeks later Jane has her accident.

Her disability coverage kicks in after 30 days, replacing two-thirds of her income. As Todd works at home most of the time anyway, he is easily able to prepare meals for Jane and to look after her, although it does take away a little from his work time. Perhaps because of this, his income doesn't rise for his second year in business, but stays at $30,000. They are somewhat disappointed, but are glad to know that Jane is improving and will soon be able to go back to work part time.

Life Change #3: Choices

After Jane's year of disability, she and Todd have to dip into their reserve fund somewhat, but were still able to contribute to their retirement savings. As soon as Jane goes back to work part time, they start to replenish the reserve account. Todd has some good contracts on the go and it looks like his income will increase substantially this year. They decide to start a family in a year.

"Financial security has a way of transforming threats into challenges and opportunities."

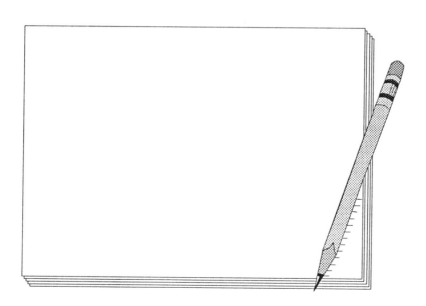

- Mike Bourcier

After one more year working at home Todd's income should be enough to support a small office outside the house, maybe a shared or packaged office. Then they can make the den into a nursery for a couple of years while Jane stays off work with the child. When she decides to go back to work they can reclaim the lower half of the house and there will be plenty of room for a family. They've had to face some challenges over the last couple of years, but Todd and Jane are pleased with what they've been able to achieve and are confident about the future.

We hope you've enjoyed these examples, but more importantly, we hope they have helped illustrate the impact of life change given one's financial position. As you can see, the couple that was content to live slightly below their means had a buffer zone so that when major changes were thrust upon them they still had choices to optimize their situation. This translated into less emotional challenge, less pressure on their marriage, and less need for compromise.

In the end, they came out way ahead of the Jones', who had lived a more glamorous lifestyle, but only for a short time.

In this changing economic and social environment, it is critical to leave yourself space to absorb change, whether it is thrust upon you or made at you own pleasure. The closer you live to your means, or the more you live beyond it, the fewer choices you will ultimately have and the lifestyle that seemed so good will ultimately entrap you and leave you treading water while others swim past.

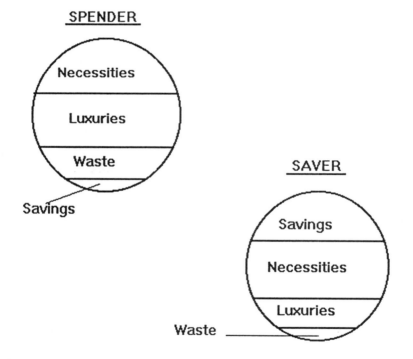

Insulating Your Financial Lifestyle Against Change

We saw in the previous section how living below your means helps lessen the impact of dramatic life change on your financial picture. It's not quite as simple as merely spending less than you make. There are many things you can do in order to protect your current situation, plan for the future, and get your money working for you.

First, create a situation where money is left at the end of the month. This may not be as hard as you think but it does involve a fundamental change in your mind-set about money. Whether consciously or unconsciously, most of us spend our money in the following priorities:

1. Necessities
2. Luxuries
3. Waste
4. Savings

Recall the definitions of these categories from the section on measuring your current financial position. Especially recall that *waste* is that "I just don't know where it went money." It just seems to disappear. Maybe it gets spent at pop machines, or lottery tickets, or turns into change and gets lost in people's cars or under the sofa. Who knows? The important thing is that you can eliminate it by changing your spending patterns to a 'pay yourself first' pattern as follows:

1. Savings
2. Necessities
3. Luxuries
4. Waste

WALKING TALL

Your savings, believe it or not, affect the way you stand, the way you walk, the tone of your voice. In short, your physical well-being and self-confidence.

A man without savings is always running. He must take the first job offered, or nearly so. He sits nervously on life's chairs because any small emergency throws him into the hands of others.

Without savings, a man must be too grateful. Gratitude is a fine thing in its place. But a constant state of gratitude is a horrible place in which to live.

A man with savings can walk tall. He may appraise opportunities in a relaxed way, have time for judicious estimates and not be rushed by economic necessity.

A man with savings can afford to resign from his job, if his "values" so dictate. And for this reason he'll never need to do so.

A man who can afford to quit is much more useful to his company, and therefore more promotable. He can afford to give his company the benefit of his most candid judgments.

A man always concerned about necessities, such as food and rent, can't afford to think in long-range career terms. He must dart to the most immediate opportunity for ready cash. Without savings, he will spend a life-time of darting, dodging.

A man with savings can afford the wonderful privilege of being generous in family or neighborhood emergencies. He can take a level stare into the eyes of any man . . . friend, stranger or enemy. It shapes his personality and character.

The ability to save has nothing to do with the size of income. Many high-income people, who spend it all, are on a tread-mill darting through life like minnows.

                                                    - H. A. McNeely

This approach forces your budget to work. In other words if your budget showed that $200 should be left over each month, then have $200 automatically taken from your bank account each month and allocated to savings and investments. In this way, that money is properly channeled from the onset. It cannot disappear on you. If your budget was somewhat accurate, you'll still easily be able to pay for necessities.

You'll probably even find that you still enjoy most or all the luxuries that you are accustomed to, because only the waste has disappeared. In most cases where we have helped people to implement this change, they have commented that they never missed that money at all.

If you complement this strategy by paying off your credit cards at the end of each month, then you are well on your way to accomplishing the first step in "insulating" your financial lifestyle.

Now that you have money left over at the end of each month the next step is to properly allocate this money in order to simultaneously create a 'buffer zone' against change and get your money working for your future.

As you recall our four examples, our wisest couple, Todd and Jane Miller, had created a fund of liquid capital to use as a reserve in case of emergencies or opportunities. It's a good idea to strive toward having at least three months net income saved in such a fund, comprised of treasury bills, term-deposits, a money market fund, or some other safe, liquid investment.

Capital Needs Analysis:
How much Life Insurance Do I Need?

Write down the total amount of income that your survivors would require per year to replace the standard of living that you currently provide for them:

(A) $_____

Now consider possible sources of capital available to produce that income:

Government provided
survivor benefits: $_____
Emergency Fund: _____
Pension Plan: _____
Saleable Assets: _____
Existing Life Insurance: _____

    Total: $_____

How much income would this capital
produce each year if invested at a
probable rate of return?   (B) $_____
(e.g.: $20,000 X 10% = $2000)

The difference between A and B is
the amount of extra income you
require from life insurance: (C) $_____

Continued on Next Page . . .

As long as you have a regular monthly amount to replenish the account, then you can feel free to use money from the fund for purchases that you feel are justified. For example, many people use this fund to accumulate their annual car insurance or travel fund. If you are planning to use the fund this way, then it is important to contribute enough each month to maintain a substantial balance. You never know when you may need it to carry you over while looking for a new job, moving, or starting a new business. People who have such a fund in place find that they have much more freedom and experience much less stress as they encounter unexpected situations in life, either positive or negative.

Todd and Jane also put something away each year toward retirement. Whether or not you expect a pension from your company, it is vital to create your own retirement savings as well. Pensions never go as far as you expect and will become less and less common anyway as society shifts toward more self-employment or contract work.

Governments of most countries provide some form of tax relief for savings that are earmarked for retirement. (E.g.. RRSP's in Canada, IRA's in the U.S.)

Take advantage of these programs, as it is always more effective to save money in a tax deferred vehicle. By not losing part of your growth each year to tax, your money will grow much more quickly. It is important to consult a financial advisor to determine what mix of investments to put your retirement fund into in order to provide the optimal balance between risk and return for your particular life situation and stage in the life cycle.

The amount of insurance you need to provide this income can be obtained by the following formula:

$$(C) / \text{probable rate of return}$$

e.g. $50,000 per year income required, divided by 10% probable return on invested money = $500,000 capital required in the form of life insurance.

Note: *This is a quick guideline only and you should discuss the matter with your financial advisor before purchasing any insurance products.*

What specific action do I have to take?

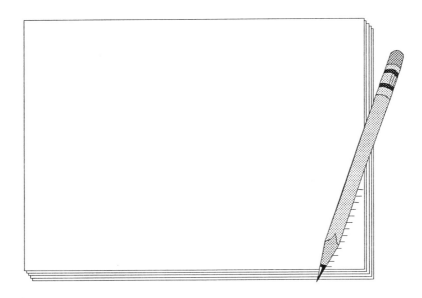

The final area to consider after allocating your financial resources is your contingency planning.

This is your protection in case you are affected by what we called in the last section a 'non-economic uncontrollable' such as a health issue or a death of an income earner. As we saw, good disability coverage allowed Todd and Jane Miller to minimize the impact of her disability on their long term plans. On the other hand, the Jones' who had no coverage saw their lives seriously compromised when Nancy Jones couldn't work for a year.

Another such uncontrollable would be a premature death. If you have people who rely on your income to support them, and if your goal is to continue supporting them, you must provide an alternate source of income if you die. Ask your financial advisor how much life insurance you would need in order to replace your income for your spouse and children.

Other possible uncontrollables you may wish to protect against include critical illness, injury or illness while traveling, and the need for permanent care either at home or in a long-term care facility.

Once you have looked after these basic areas you will have created a nice 'financial buffer zone' that will protect you from the potential negative impacts of change on your lifestyle and peace of mind.

The Man in the Glass

When you get what you want in your struggle for wealth,
And the world makes you king for a day,
Just go to the mirror and look at yourself
And see what the man has to say.

For it isn't your father or mother or wife,
Whose judgment upon you must pass,
The person whose verdict counts most in your life
Is the one staring back from the glass.

He's the fellow to please, never mind all the rest,
For he's with you clear up to the end.
And you've passed your most dangerous, difficult test
If the man in the glass is your friend.

You may be like Jack Horner and chisel a plum
And think you're a wonderful guy.
But the man in the glass says you're only a bum
If you can't look him straight in the eye.

You may fool the whole world down the pathway of years
And get pats on the back as you pass
But your final reward will be heartaches and tears
If you've cheated the man in the glass.

- Unknown

Implementing Change

In this section, we have talked about some of the key components of financial planning and how to integrate those into a plan that you can stick to and that will help you deal with the rapidly changing social and economic environment around us today. We introduced tools to measure your own current position, we explored the impacts of change on various possible financial situations and looked at ways to modify or fine-tune your situation to benefit from positive change and insulate you against negative change.

Sit back now and contemplate what you have read on finances integrating it with the material from earlier in the book. You may find as a result that your financial situation no longer measures up to your expectations and that you wish to make some changes.

Implementing financial change is much like implementing change in any other area of your life. Consider your core values and beliefs and look at how your current financial situation and aspirations correlate to those values and beliefs. Many of us find that our financial objectives are out of sync with our values. Maybe we assumed that the way our parents made decisions was the right way for us as well. Maybe we were motivated by keeping up with the Jones'. Maybe we simply hadn't given much thought to what we wanted in the long run.

Or maybe this has reaffirmed that you are happy with your present lifestyle. Whatever the case, it never hurts to do a little review from time to time. If you need help with your review, please feel free to send us an E-mail.

"The masters in the art of living make little distinction between their work and their play, their labor and their leisure, their information, their recreation, their love and their religion. They hardly know which is which. They simply pursue their vision of excellence at whatever they do, leaving others to decide whether they are working or playing."

- James Michener

SIMPLIFYING YOUR LIFE

Looking back, we often say "Life was so simple then."

If life no longer feels simple, perhaps we complicated it ourselves. We all started life with the same basic needs: air, food, shelter and love still top the list of things we need, whatever our sex, age and education.

As time went on, our list grew. The first few things we wanted, in addition to the basics, were the toys that others had, then the cars and homes that others had, followed by attractive conveniences such as cable TV, a microwave and an endless list of household and kitchen gadgets that most of us own but rarely use.

Then the list grew even more to include a second car and a satellite dish to capture 125 channels of programming on our Big Screen TVs. But all this did not satisfy us, the pursuit of bigger, better and more prompted us to buy a second house that we called "a vacation cottage" and of course the boat that "has" to come with it, otherwise, what's the point?

Then the "travel bug" hit us and we needed to spend time abroad. Of course at that time, we did not go to the cottage anymore as we did not have enough time. How did life become so complicated?

Many people reach a point where they need to have two or three jobs just to pay for all the toys they no longer have time to enjoy because they are working too hard to pay for them. Does that sound familiar?

"It's good to have money
and the things
money can buy,

but it's good too to
check up and be
sure you haven't lost the
things money can't buy."

- George Horace Lorimer

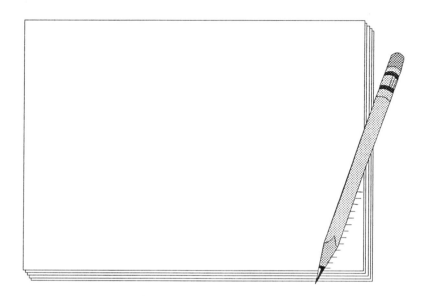

We do not set out to complicate life, we create our complexities one bit at a time without noticing the erosion of our freedom. Then, we wake up. Not only does the financial perspective hit us where it hurts but the intricate maintenance of this lifestyle kills the pleasure that it should bring.

My idea of a good time is not about spending five hours a week cutting grass or two weeks of vacation repainting the house every year. Now, I realize that this is a matter of taste and choice. For the handyman, home improvement can be a thrill.

For many of us, this craziness ends when our children leave home. Then, we sell the big house, settle in a much smaller space where our "toys" don't fit, so we get rid of them. We unload. What a relief! Moving is really a good wake-up call, when you open the cupboards and start wrapping things you haven't even looked at in five years.

Our message to you is: UNLOAD NOW!

When Michèle and I decided to take the big step and simplify our life, we devoted all our energy to this goal. It took us less than six months but we warn you, not everyone is comfortable moving that quickly. Do it at your own pace, but start now!

If you are too young to have accumulated all this stuff…"beware!"

We found our simplification extremely rewarding. Here is what we achieved in that time frame:

"Too many people spend money they haven't earned, to buy things they don't want, to impress people they don't like."

- Will Rogers

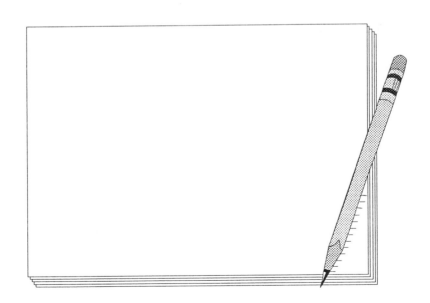

Moved from a four-bedroom house to a one-bedroom apartment

Got rid of the BMW and the payments that came with it

Stopped paying for other people who badly needed to fly on their own

Sold everything we had except for our clothes, two computers, our books and a TV

Moved from Eastern Canada to British Columbia and bought a new, more affordable car

Dropped a very lucrative business which had become boring and started a new challenging business on the West Coast

Finally sold the house back East, at a MAJOR financial loss

Bought a small log-house two hours away from Vancouver, relocated there ...and started writing this book.

The result, our financial requirement to make ends meet is about 20% of what it used to be. This allows us to be free. We do not need as much revenue from our business which, in turn, allows us to choose our assignments and our clients and provides us with more time to write. Our clients are happy because we are more available when **we decide** to work with them.

"You mean to tell me that you can take responsibility for an $80million project and you can't plan 2 weeks a year to go off with your family and have fun?"

- Lee Iacocca... to a manager

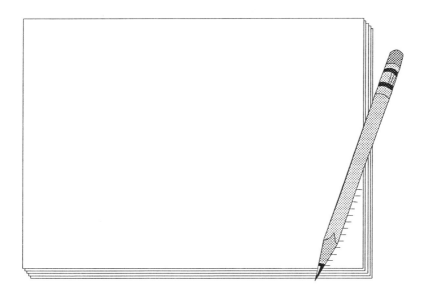

We are happier because we truly enjoy what we do.

We also have more personal time for the things that matter to us and mesh with our values.

We allow more time for our relationship and for other wonderful new friendships that have developed along the way.

We identified the people, situations and activities that energized us and gave them our top priority. Living close to nature was a strong need for both of us, thus the log house. We chose to live here because our home and environment fill us with positive energy and fit our simple lifestyle. We did tremendous soul-searching before we felt confident that our business would continue to thrive in a non-traditional setting and that we would follow the path we have designed for our future.

From our cabin in the wilderness, we lead the activities of a group of professional consultants located in twenty countries. In addition, we serve "on-site" clients in Vancouver and Seattle. Furthermore, we deliver "live" seminars all over North-America and Europe and finally, we support this book with our network of associates. This is what the 21st century holds for us.

Back to simplifying **your life**. Again, what works for us may not fit your needs. You reflected on your values and beliefs. You have set goals and prepared your passport to the future.

"The best test of the quality
of a civilization is
the quality of its
leisure."

- Irwin Edman

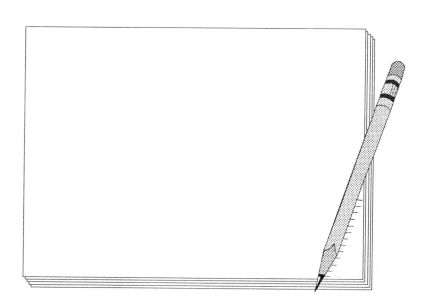

You are aware of the need for continuous training. You learned how to create and maintain a high energy level and how to use financial resources judiciously in the process. All these solutions came from you, we were merely guiding you to put them on paper.

Likewise, our approach to life simplification is drastic and might not fit your own value system or beliefs. Please take what you need now and re-assess your needs from time to time.

In fact, we encourage you to send us your ideas for simplifying life. You will benefit from the input by all the people who choose to access all our resources on the Internet and share their experiences. Let us know what works for you, share the rewards you reaped.

The first step

Begin by putting time aside to re-evaluate your life.

This, for some, will mean going away for a weekend in a high-energy place to really examine their life more closely. For others, it will simply mean setting aside an hour a day for a week to sit down and seriously take a fresh look at everything you do and all your possessions.

Whatever works for you, commit to do it NOW! Start immediately with the following exercises.

254

Useless stuff list:

Things	# months	Next use
_____	_____	_____
_____	_____	_____
_____	_____	_____
_____	_____	_____
_____	_____	_____
_____	_____	_____
_____	_____	_____
_____	_____	_____
_____	_____	_____
_____	_____	_____
_____	_____	_____
_____	_____	_____
_____	_____	_____
_____	_____	_____
_____	_____	_____
_____	_____	_____

The useless stuff list

On the opposite page, list all the items you have not used for the past year. Write down the number of months you have not used these things on each line. Walk around your house if necessary, open cupboards, spend some time in the basement, in the attic, in the garage.

What about clothes? When we moved, we filled five large boxes with clothes, not stuff that was in boxes in the attic, but clothing from our bedroom. We've yet to miss anything. And even a year later, we don't feel compelled to buy ourselves new wardrobes. The things that may come back in style, the "skinny wardrobe", you will wear one day, donate them to the needy people or sell them at a consignment store. Ridding yourself of excess belongings is tremendously freeing.

Now, take a close look at your list and ask yourself why those items have gone untouched. Perhaps you haven't had the time to enjoy the hobbies you once did. Perhaps the fishing equipment has sat in the closet because you've been too busy working. If fishing is something you value, hang on to the gear. Now you just may find the time. On the other hand, you most likely have amassed piles of items you no longer value.

Then, in the third column, write down a date at which you think you will use these "things". For items such as "vaporizers" which you hope not to use because it will mean you are sick, just write "Emergency". If you cannot think of ever using the item again, sell it or give it away but SIMPLIFY.

Stuff I have for other people to use

Things	For whom / Why I keep it
_____	_____
_____	_____
_____	_____
_____	_____
_____	_____
_____	_____
_____	_____
_____	_____
_____	_____
_____	_____
_____	_____
_____	_____
_____	_____
_____	_____
_____	_____
_____	_____
_____	_____

Be careful with books and music CDs. We all keep books when they are read (maybe too many). We have a very large library at home but it is for research. (I guess we can rationalize anything.) By the way, how many items did you write down? Did you think of all the stuff at your parents' house, in the attic or the garage?

The accommodating list

On the opposite page, list all the items you keep for other people to use. In this category goes the extra bedroom, the extra towels and linen. The extra bicycle or shovel. Some of these items might be on the first list, but you may write them here, too. Maybe they are not on the first list because you thought that they were used in the last year, but not by you. If you are keeping a sewing machine because your daughter borrows it once a year, give it to her!

Don't forget all the paraphernalia that people did not return, such as the lawnmower or the sun lamp you loaned to a friend. Taking a look at this list, can you explain what makes you so accommodating?

Why do you buy and keep stuff for others? If "accommodating others" ranks high in your value system, ignore this advice, otherwise, SIMPLIFY.

Get off the automatic-pilot

Simplifying doesn't only mean ridding ourselves of what we don't need and reducing our expenses. It also means a simpler lifestyle. As humans, we favor routines and repetitive activities.

Things I have been doing on "auto-pilot"

"Auto-Pilot"   **How can I change it?**

_____	_____
_____	_____
_____	_____
_____	_____
_____	_____
_____	_____
_____	_____
_____	_____
_____	_____
_____	_____
_____	_____
_____	_____
_____	_____
_____	_____
_____	_____

For example, if we have been shopping for food on Thursday night for years, we tend to head to the market on auto-pilot, never reconsidering if another time would be more convenient or pleasant.

The brain is conditioned. "It is Thursday night let's shop for food." We know that this is a bad time because the stores are crowded and we hate line-ups, so why not slow down for a minute and figure out a better way.

Using the opposite page, list the things you do without thinking. This is a trick question and a difficult one. If you do these things on auto-pilot, you probably don't notice your behavior.

Can you come up with any automatic behaviors? These are time grabbers of the worst kind. They are subconscious so they are hard to identify. Go over your week, what do you do over and over again, what activities have become routine. What about weekends?

Work habits are another automatic behavior. We prefer working mornings and nights and saving the afternoons for social activities. People who work at home will tell you that they achieve more on a broken schedule than by having to think in accordance with a clock.

We seek comfort in the familiar. We don't have to think much, there is no great risk involved. Try deliberately incorporating breathing space into your schedule. Ask yourself over and over again:

I wish I had more time so I could

_____
_____
_____
_____
_____
_____
_____
_____

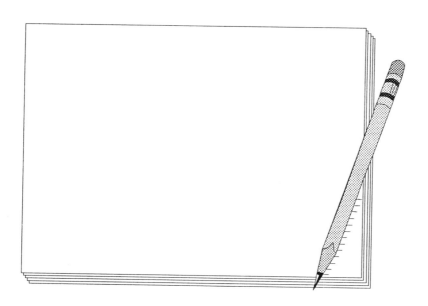

Do I really want to do this?
Do I really want to see this person?
What would happen if I worked from home today?

Now, complete this sentence:
"I wish I had more time so that I could...................."

How would you spend that extra time? I know many people
who swear that they cannot find a half-an hour a day to read
a book or take a walk alone. Free up time so that you can
do what you REALLY want to do.

Returning to our value system. If we listed relationships as
most important in our lives, we must keep in mind that
relationships, important ones, require quality time. We
should treat them with the respect we accord them in
theory. They, unfortunately are very often the first to suffer
the "not enough time" syndrome. So, **free up time** and
spend it where it counts.

There are many ways to free up time. For instance, look at
your schedule and realize that perhaps you've played bridge
each week for the past year, but you no longer look forward
to the game. You've continued to play out of habit and a
desire to not let down your companions. But you've got
decisions to make. UNLOAD! Learn to say NO!

Perhaps you spend Saturdays cleaning the house. If you
have a family, are they doing their share? If all your family
members did their share, maybe a little bit every day, you
could end up with freeing your Saturdays or a big part of
them... UNLOAD! Make a schedule and make sure the
tasks are distributed fairly.

"We first make our
habits and then our
habits make us."

- John Dryden

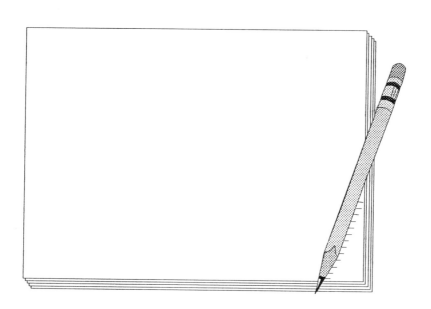

Things you do for others

Parents of young children can really associate with this one. We call them "Soccer Moms" or "Taxi Dads." I know so many people that have no time for themselves because they spend a few hours each day chauffeuring their kids to all kinds of activities.

We agree that kids need activities and a social life, but not at the expense of their parents' free time. We live in a society that puts children in charge. Many parents are becoming slaves to their kids. Does that yield a better child?

We believe that many children have too many activities, their every minute is regimented. They suffer the "not enough time syndrome" before hitting puberty.

It was so simple then... Remember your own youth, the carefree summers... Many children will not have such memories, they are already out of breath at age 12. Help them SIMPLIFY their lives as well.

Kids can choose among activities that require the presence of parents or a lift to and from the event. Lord knows that we would not suggest to send our youngsters on the street by themselves at night in our cities. But choice is something that kids have to learn and they also have to acknowledge that their parents have a life and respect their time the same way they want theirs respected.

"It takes more intelligence to
live a simple life
than to let life take
over our
intelligence."

- Mike Bourcier

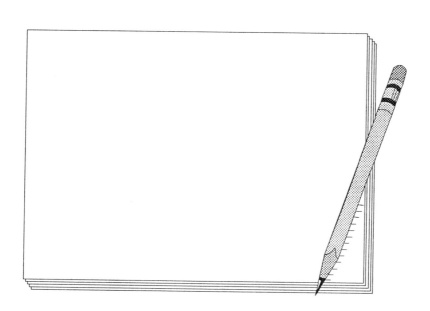

Ask one of your children to spend time helping around the house and in too many cases, you will hear, "I don't have time." Harsh as it sounds, you just might retort that, "If you don't have time for me. I don't have time for you." What's wrong with allowing a certain amount of your time to these kids' activities and let them choose how they want to use that time? If your primary value is family, is your goal to raise children who become responsible adults? If you value your children's future, you will agree that discipline and choices are paramount.

Guess what, it does not get any easier after the kids leave home. You will eventually get to the point where your own parents impose time constraints on you. The same rule applies: If you do not ask for respect, you won't get it.

Do not accept that people abuse YOUR time. I have a single rule of thumb, if you set up a meeting and don't show-up, you don't get another chance without a reasonable excuse. We can't keep people waiting and expect them to accept our behavior. Their time is as important as ours. If you're unavoidably detained, phone ahead and say so. That's simple enough!

How does attention to promptness fit in with simplifying your life? Your time is precious and if you want to put your plan in action and reach your goals, you cannot afford people sabotaging your schedule. We agree that relaxation is important, but not when somebody else is waiting.

"Time is the only
non-renewable resource we
have and the only
one most of us
can't manage."

- Unknown

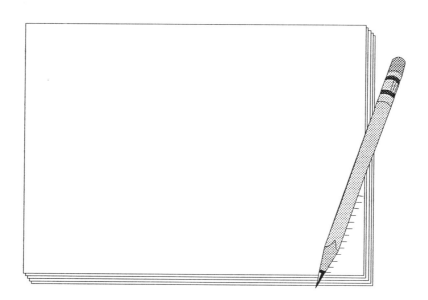

I told an important client recently that I would not type a fairly large text that he wanted me to include in another document I was preparing for his company. I do not think that this is a good use of my time, and besides, I don't like typing. I am sure that the client ended up saving a substantial amount of money by hiring a proficient typist. In the end we are both more happy.

Don't go to work

Let work come to you, if you can. With today's technology more and more jobs fit the "telecommuting" environment. If you do not have to go to work, don't. It will most likely be only a few days a week but every hour not spent in traffic is worth two.

You can now use the time to learn and activate your plan. You can achieve more because you have an opportunity to work during your peak productive hours. If you can achieve more in less time, doesn't that simplify your life?

If you are self-employed, take a good look at what you do and ask yourself if you really need a full-time office. We decided to work from home many years ago, and honestly, even if someone offered us the most beautiful office space for FREE, we would pass.

In our case, frequent travel and seminars prevent us from feeling isolated. For some of you, the fear of loneliness might keep you from unloading the office. Just remember, you can maintain an active professional life and still work at home.

"If you are not
working at home
already, you will."

- Frank Ogden

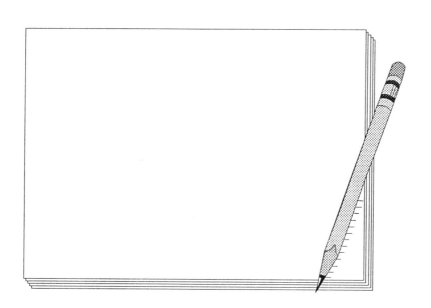

Be creative

Who said that work has to last from 9 a.m. to 5 p.m. Monday through Friday? Actually, you can expect that in the future, work hours will be less structured. Job sharing and part-time employment will contribute to more flexible schedules. Create your own schedule. Yes, even in a large corporation, you can change the way things are done.

We recently helped a friend, a new mother, who could hardly afford going back to work with the cost of day care. She is a telephone receptionist for a large multinational. We approached her employer with the idea to have her answer the phone at home three days-a-week, an option the company had not considered. Since her physical presence was unnecessary, the company agreed and suggested it to other employees.

In the process, the firm resolved a problem with the lunch time back-ups. Now, a fair amount of the workforce does their jobs during broken shifts from home. Virtually everybody is happier.

We mentioned earlier that in the future, people will be paid for what they know and what they can contribute to an organization rather than for the number of hours they sit at a desk. Can this knowledge help SIMPLIFY YOUR LIFE? How much more time would you devote to your plan of action?

How much time would you save only by avoiding traveling to and from the office? Maybe you can take an extra 20 minutes a day for that exercise program...

"In a rapidly changing environment, the specialist can become obsolete overnight."

- Frank Ogden

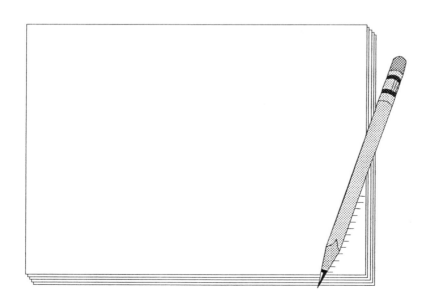

Use technology

Simplifying your life does not mean eating food from a microwave every day even if the microwave is very useful. What else did advances in technology bring us that can SIMPLIFY our lives?

Bank machines and bank cards (direct debit) have greatly enhanced our utilization of time. Earlier, we criticized the habit of careless spending with convenience cards. But used thoughtfully, debit cards can save you a tremendous amount of time. You do not have to go to the bank, you are safer on the street as you do not carry cash, and you avoid credit card debt.

For a large group of readers, you already know that the computer, especially E-mail, saves you all kinds of time and money with instant transfer of information and documents across the world or across the street at a ridiculously low cost. We pay our bills by E-mail. We receive bills by E-mail (nothing is perfect). We send birthday cards for less than the price of a postage stamp. If you are not connected yet, consider taking the time to learn. Make it a priority, buy a computer if you do not have one. It will pay for itself in six months. A computer will SIMPLIFY your life in so many ways.

One word of warning about computers. If you continually strive to acquire the latest technology, save yourself the trouble. Just go into receivership now. We don't know anybody who remains on top of field equipment. When we bought our Pentium 60 in January 1995, we believed we had the latest and greatest. That lasted about 30 days.

"I think this is a wonderful time to be alive. There are never been so many opportunities to do things that were impossible before."

- Bill Gates

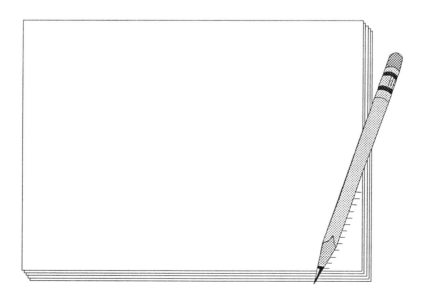

This book has been produced with that computer, and we still rely on it as our main business system, but others are now more advanced. Do not get caught into buying the best, buy what you need. You need not spend your life's savings on a computer. You can purchase a modest system for under $1,200 and your connection to the Internet should not run more than $10 or $15 monthly.

Once you are connected, you can save money by locating the best price for any products or services. If you do not want to pay "on-line" because you fear hackers invading your privacy, you can still find what you need. By the way, if you do not trust financial transactions by credit or debit card on the Net, please be consistent in your thinking. The next time you reserve a hotel room or you give your card to a waiter in a restaurant, think about it! You are more exposed there than on the Net. Anyway, you can save HOURS and significant DOLLARS shopping on-line.

As it is for us, once you set your mind to it, simplifying your life will become an ongoing process. It ties in with giving priority of time and energy to what we value most. It means letting go of the things, activities and self-imposed obligations that clutter our lives without adding anything significant to our happiness or well being. As you advance on this journey, we invite you to share what works for you and experiment with what has worked for others using the Learning@living site.

EPILOGUE

History has demonstrated that the greatest dreams are often born in periods of greatest distress. Personal crisis shake us and force us to find new solutions and approaches to life.

We don't pretend to have found the perfect way to live for everybody. We have found what works for us NOW and shared our journey with you.

We do not cast a judgment on people who chose to live to work. At certain times in our separate lives, Michèle and I have used work as a buoy to maintain our sanity in a world that seemed to collapse around us. On the other hand we do not believe that "living to work" should become a permanent life goal for anybody.

If our approach helped you we have reached our objective in publishing this book. If you can share your experience with us and others, we will all be richer.

Mike and Michèle

ABOUT "Learning@living"

"Learning@living" is more than a book. It is your personal assistant to face tomorrow's challenges in earning a living and simplifying your life.

Our WWW site (**www.living-icic.com**) was designed to host the book and allow unlimited growth stimulated by our research and YOUR input.

We invite you to keep in touch by E-mail as much as you want (**learning@living-icic.com**). We will do our best to get back to all of you individually and answer your questions. We would also like to get your comments and suggestions as they will help us and others in developing our resources.

You can consult our site to find out how you can maintain access after the initial "free access" period has expired.

We will present **conferences, seminars and workshops** on "Learning@living" all over the USA, Canada and Europe. If you wish to be aware of our schedule, you will be able to find that information on our site when it becomes available. If you prefer, send us an E-mail with the words "seminar schedule" in the body of the text. We will include you on our E-mailing list.

You can reach us by FAX at (604)869-3864 but we really prefer E-mail.

Mike and Michèle

You read the book...
now hear them speak.

Mike and Michèle are among the most dynamic
speakers in North America today.
They deliver keynote addresses, speeches, lectures,
lead discussions, host executive retreats and
conduct seminars
adapted to any needs.

In addition, they are retained as advisors by major
Corporations and Governments around the world to
assist them in dealing with the phenomenal rate of
change and its impact on people.

For information about how to book
a personal appearance, in house training or
to discuss their services please contact them
directly by **FAX** (604)869-3864
or E-mail (learning@living-icic.com)